Theology 122
Foundation Doctrines

An

Oral Learners Bible Institute

Course

Written by: Rev. Robb Hawks

olBi *is a ministry of the Oral Learners Initiative, one of the International Ministries of the Assemblies of God World Missions.*

 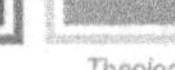      

The Oral Learners Bible Institute was created to train and equip men and women, to plant and pastor churches around the world. This training is designed for oral learners, who learn by listening to stories. Thus, each lesson is designed to be produced on video which the student can see and hear. Oral learners are also referred to as "narrative" learners. Everyone is born a narrative learner. Traditional education is designed to teach a child "higher critical thinking," where information is taught through organized outline and lecture. Narrative thinkers, however, learn through stories or narratives.

Each lesson of the Oral Learners Bible Institute focuses on one truth, which is typically drawn out of a Bible story. Lessons also include oral questions and their correct answers, and an assignment to help the student apply the lesson to his or her life.

The lessons presented in this book are the actual English "scripts," which are now being translated into numerous languages. They are then presented on camera by native speakers of the language, to create the olBi course, *Theology 122-Foundation Doctrines*.

This theology course will walk the student through the six foundation doctrines listed in Hebrews chapter 6. These six doctrines are the basic or "foundational" doctrines of the Christian faith.

CONTENTS

1 Introduction

People build houses in different ways. Some people build with wood. Others use stone or bricks. Many homes today are built from concrete blocks. No matter how the house is built, there is one thing that all houses need if the builder expects the house to remain. Every house needs a good foundation to build upon.

My life and your life are like houses. We build our lives with knowledge, relationships, and life experiences. But our lives, just like a house, must have a good foundation. In this course we will learn what the Bible teaches are the foundational or basic doctrines of Christianity. There is a book in the Bible called 'Hebrews.' It was a letter written to Hebrew Christians, laying out a broad foundation of teaching about Jesus Christ. It was written from a Hebrew perspective so that the Jewish readers could easily understand the principles being taught.

The author of the Book of Hebrews wrote: "Therefore leaving the elementary teaching about the Christ, let us press on to maturity, not laying again a foundation of repentance from dead works and of faith toward God, of instruction about washings, and laying on of hands, and the resurrection of the dead, and eternal judgment" (Heb 6:1-2). From this we learn that there are six elementary or foundational doctrines that every Christian should understand. These six foundational doctrines will be taught in this course. Every pastor should include lessons on these six doctrines in his teaching to his congregation.

The first doctrine is "repentance from dead works." Repentance is the first and foremost step in the life of every Christian.

"Faith toward God" is also a requirement for becoming a Christian. One must, of course, believe that God exists before one can come to him.

Third, the doctrine of "washings," or "baptisms," includes water baptism and the baptism in the Holy Spirit.

"Laying on of hands" covers a number of important aspects of ministry within the church.

Christians do not live without hope. We have been promised that every Christian who dies will be raised from the dead. This is the fifth doctrine, "resurrection."

Finally, there will be a day when everyone who has ever lived will stand before God. Each will be judged for their lives and actions. This is "eternal judgment."

Let's say these six foundation doctrines together. Please repeat after me: Repentance   Faith   Baptisms Laying on of Hands   Resurrection   Eternal Judgment (Pause)
Let's say these six foundation doctrines again. Please repeat after me: Repentance   Faith   Baptisms Laying on of Hands   Resurrection   Eternal Judgment (Pause)

Every person building a house understands the importance of having a good foundation. Jesus himself told a story about two men who decided to build houses.

"Therefore, everyone who hears these words of mine and acts on them, may be compared to a wise man who built his house on the rock. And the rain fell, and the floods came, and the winds blew and slammed against that house; and *yet* it did not fall, for it had been founded on the rock. Everyone who hears these words of mine and does not act on them, will be like a foolish man who built his house on the sand. The rain fell, and the floods came, and the winds blew and slammed against that house; and it fell. And great was its fall" (Matt 7:24-27).

The "rock" is Christ himself and his teachings. The crowds who heard this story were amazed at Jesus' teaching. He taught as one who had divine authority. He said that a wise person would not only hear, but also obey what they had heard him say. In this course you will learn the foundational teachings of Jesus Christ. You will be encouraged to put them into practice as you build a strong foundation for your life and ministry. Faith in Christ the rock brings about changed lives, established firmly on him.

This lesson is **important** because it teaches the six foundation doctrines of Christianity.

The **main truth** of this lesson is that the six foundational teachings in Hebrews will help every Christian to lay a firm foundation upon which to build their lives.

Let us **review** this lesson by answering the following questions:

1. We learned that the author of the Book of Hebrews said that there are six foundation doctrines to Christianity. What are the first three doctrines?
	A. If you said, "Repentance, faith, and baptisms," then you are correct.

2. Can you name the next three foundation doctrines?
	A. If you said, "Laying on of hands, resurrection, and eternal judgment," you are correct.

3. Jesus told the story of a man who built his house upon the rock. What happened when the storm came against the house built upon the rock?

      A. If you said that it withstood the storm, you are right.

Your **assignment** for this lesson is to quote the list of six foundation doctrines at least ten times until you have memorized the list.

2 Repentance: Godly Sorrow

I once heard about a man who had a violent temper. When he got drunk, he would become violent and would beat his wife and children. After he got sober, he would feel remorse. Then he would tell his family that he was sorry for what he had done to them. And for a time, things would be good. But then he would get drunk again, become violent, injuring his family again. This man was sorry for what he did, but his sorrow did not lead to any change in his behavior.

In our first lesson we learned that there are six basic or foundational doctrines that every Christian should know. These doctrines are: Repentance, Faith, Baptisms, Laying on of Hands, Resurrection, and Eternal Judgment. In this lesson we will begin to explore concepts of repentance.

What does it mean to repent? One definition says, to repent is "to feel or express sincere regret or remorse about one's wrongdoing or sin." Indeed, sorrow is important to repentance. But there is actually much more to repentance that just feeling sorry for your actions. The apostle Paul wrote this about repentance: "For the **sorrow** that is according to *the will of* God produces a repentance without regret, *leading* to salvation, but the **sorrow** of the world produces death" (2Cor 7:10).

So, what is the difference between Godly sorrow that leads to repentance and worldly sorrow that produces death? There is a very good example of worldly sorrow in the story of King Saul and David.

Now after the Israelites conquered the land of Canaan, there was no king over the people. It was God's intent that the people would look to him as their king. Thus, God gave to the people prophets to lead them and wise leaders to serve as judges within the land. For hundreds of years the people of Israel lived this way. Some of the leaders were very godly; others drifted away from God and led the people into sin. So, God would have to raise up a new godly leader to bring the people back to him. The prophet Samuel was one such man that God raised up to restore the people to himself.

It was during the time that Samuel was prophet that the people of Israel began to complain. "All of the lands around us have kings to lead them, but we do not!" They grumbled to each other. This did not please God. He knew that kings were not always the best leaders of nations. Finally, the grumbling and complaining became so great that God decided to let them have a king. He knew only one way the people would learn the value of having God as their king. He would let them be led by an earthly king. Soon a tall, handsome, young man named Saul was anointed to be the first king of Israel.

At first Saul tried to follow God's commands, but disobedience broke his relationship with God. This led to his being tormented in his mind. Then Israel's enemies, the Philistines, prepared themselves for war. Now the Philistines had a three-meter-tall giant as their champion. All of Israel was afraid to go out and face him. But a young shepherd boy named David, who was anointed by God, went out and killed the giant. He used only a sling and a smooth stone. All of Israel rejoiced at David's victory. So King Saul brought David back to his home to be part of the royal court (1Sam 17).

Now the presence of God was upon David and he could play the lyre and sing beautifully. Whenever he played and sang before the King, Saul found moments of peace. But Saul knew that God was no longer with him, but that God's anointing was upon David. This, plus the fact that the people loved David more than the king, led Saul to great jealousy. One day David was playing and singing for Saul, whose mind was greatly tormented. Saul was walking around in his house with a spear in his hand. Suddenly Saul stopped and threw the spear at David, trying to kill him! David escaped without harm and hid from the king.

This jealousy would lead King Saul to try to kill David on many different occasions. But David would never raise his hand against the king. Instead, he continued to serve in the king's army, fighting the king's enemies. Finally, King Saul earnestly set out to kill David, and this forced him to flee for his life. David gathered around himself a small group of friends. They became a raiding band of warriors who fought against Israel's enemies.

One day King Saul got news of where they were hiding in the wilderness. He gathered together an army of 3,000 soldiers and set off to find David and kill him. After journeying many hours into the wilderness, King Saul need to find a place to empty his bladder and bowels. There was a cave on the side of the mountain ridge and Saul entered into the cave for privacy. He set his weapons down, removed his sword belt, and finally laid aside his royal cloak. Then, lifting his tunic, he squatted to relieve himself. Unknown to the king, the cave he had chosen was the very cave where David and his band of soldiers were hiding. David's men wanted to kill the king, who at that moment was totally defenseless. But David refused to lift up his hand against the king. Instead he crept up to where the king had dropped his royal robe and cut off a piece of its edge. Saul finished relieving himself and, after dressing, returned to his men. David then went and stood at the entrance to the cave and called out to the king.

"My king, why do you seek to kill me? Who has lied to you and said that I am disloyal. Look! I have in my hand the edge from your very robe. I could easily have taken your life, but I am your loyal servant."

King Saul suddenly felt great sorrow and wept for his behavior. "David my son, you are a better man than me. What man allows his enemy to escape his hand? You have dealt me a great kindness." And so Saul and his army left David and returned to their city. But David and his men went up into the mountains (1Sam 24).

Now it seemed that King Saul had repented of his behavior and would no longer seek to kill David. But the sorrow that he experienced was short lived. He was not sorrowful that he was trying to kill David. Rather, he was full of sorrow that he could have been killed and that David had spared his life. This again proved that David was a more righteous man than the king. Saul was now forced to return the kindness to David or he would lose face in front of his army. But, sometime later it was again revealed to King Saul where David and his men were hiding. Again, Saul took an army to go and kill David. But the Lord caused a deep sleep to fall upon Saul and his army that night. David and a few of his men sneaked into Saul's camp. Again, David's men wanted to kill the king, but David would not allow it. Instead David took the king's spear and the jug of water that was near the king's head and then they left. The next morning David stood on the hillside and called out to the king and his generals.

"You have not done a good job protecting the king. Men sneaked into the camp last night and could have taken his life." David shouted.

"Is that you David?" The king asked.

"It is me. Look, I have the king's spear and the water jug that was by his head. I could have taken his life, but I have never done anything against the king."

Then the king said, "I have sinned. Return, my son David, for I will not harm you again, because my life was precious in your sight this day."

Again, the king and his army departed. But David knew better than to return to Israel. The king had many times expressed sorrow and even admitted he was wrong. But the king never changed. He always tried to kill David again. Thus, David and his men fled the land of Israel (1Sam 26).

Soon King Saul was again tormented in his mind and felt sorry for trying to kill David. He called for him to come back and play for him. Earlier David had returned to the king. But King Saul's sorrow was not a godly sorrow. It did not lead to true repentance and a change in heart and behavior. It was a worldly sorrow. King Saul felt sorrow for his behavior only because it deprived him of David's singing. His desire to have David return was not to restore their relationship, but rather to meet his own selfish needs. You can imagine the end result of worldly sorrow. It is temporary and does not lead to true repentance. Indeed, King Saul would pursue David and try to kill him on a number of different occasions. After each attempt on David's life, Saul would feel sorrow and remorse, but never for the motives behind his actions. His sorrow never led to a change in behavior.

This lesson is **important** because it demonstrates the connection between sorrow for our behavior and repentance.

The **main truth** of this lesson is that without godly sorrow there will be no true repentance, which is made evident by a change in behavior.

To **review** this lesson, answer the following questions:

1. King Saul chased David and his men into the wilderness to kill them. While hiding in a cave David had a chance to kill Saul but chose not to. When King Saul was confronted with this, what emotion did he experience?
 A. If you said, "Sorrow," you are correct.

2. King Saul experienced sorrow when David spared his life. How do we know that this sorrow did not lead to true repentance?
 A. If you said that King Saul tried to kill David again, then you are correct.

3. Godly sorrow will lead to what?
 A. If you said, "True repentance," then you are correct.

Your **assignment** for this lesson is to listen to it two or three more times, until you can tell the story of King Saul and David to someone else. Ask, "Is sorrow for being caught in an act the same as repenting for that act?" As you share the difference between worldly sorrow and true repentance, prayerfully ask God to show you and your fellow believers if there are sins you need to truly repent of.

3 Repentance: Confession of Sin

The first president of the United States of America was George Washington. An American folk tale says that when he was a child, he took an axe and cut down a cherry tree. As the story goes, his father confronted him and asked, "George, did you cut down my cherry tree?"

Little George confessed, "I cannot tell a lie. I cut down the cherry tree!"

Confession is a very important part of repentance. We must first admit or confess our sin in order to truly repent. In our last lesson we learned the difference between worldly sorrow and godly sorrow. Today we will learn how confession can be an important part of true repentance.

The ancient city of Ephesus was once one of the major cities of the Greek and then Roman empires. Today the ruins of Ephesus can be found in the country of Turkey. Fifty thousand people lived in Ephesus during the time of Jesus and the apostle Paul. It was famous for the temple to the Greek goddess Artemis. This temple was considered one of the "Seven Wonders of the Ancient World." The people of Ephesus were very proud of it.

It was to this bustling city of commerce that the apostle Paul came to preach the gospel. When he arrived, he discovered that there were already disciples in the city. He began talking to them. He discovered that they had been baptized in water, but had never been baptized in the Holy Spirit. Paul told them, "John's baptism was a baptism of repentance. John told the people to believe in the one coming after him, that is, in Jesus." Upon hearing this, all of the disciples believed in Jesus and were baptized in Jesus' name. Then Paul placed his hands upon them. They were filled with the Holy Spirit and began to speak in tongues.

This began two years of ministry by Paul in the city of Ephesus.

Paul began to preach and teach in the Jewish synagogue. For three months he argued powerfully that Jesus was the Messiah. But he met stiff resistance from some of the Jewish leaders, so he took the disciples and left the synagogue. He began to preach and teach in the lecture hall of Tyrannus. All of the Jews and Greeks who lived in Ephesus and the surrounding villages heard the word of the Lord during Paul's time in Ephesus. God performed many great miracles through Paul during his ministry there. People were cured of their illnesses and evil spirits left them.

Now there were some Jews who went around attempting to drive out evil spirits. These were the seven sons of the Jewish chief priest named Sceva. These men had heard that many evil spirits were being driven out through the ministry of Paul. So, they decided that they would try to use Paul's method, to be more successful in their business of freeing people from demonic spirits. One day they were hired to drive an evil spirit out of a man. They demanded that the evil spirit leave the man by saying, "In the name of the Jesus whom Paul preaches, I command you to come out."

The evil spirit answered them, "Jesus I know, and Paul I know about, but who are you?" The man who had the evil spirit jumped on them and overpowered them all. He gave them such a beating that they fled from the house. They were bruised and bleeding, with their clothing torn from their bodies.

News of this quickly spread through the city and soon both Jews and Greeks began to fear and respect the name of Jesus. Now there were those who had come to believe in Jesus that came forward to confess their sins. Some of these had practiced sorcery and witchcraft. These people had privately used spells and magic rituals to try to change people. Although believers in Christ, they still held onto their books of sorcery. They believed, but had not truly repented of their past lives. These believers experienced godly sorrow and then came forward and confessed to their witchcraft. They brought out their scrolls of sorcery—rolls of parchment with written secrets—and publicly burned them. When the value of these scrolls was added up it came to the equivalent of the annual wages for 150 people (Acts 19:1-20).

There are many things that can be learned from this story. Perhaps most important is that these people, who experienced Godly sorrow, were willing to suffer the shame of publicly confessing their sins. Their confession led to true repentance. The proof of their repentance is that they were willing, at great personal cost, to destroy the very items that bound them to sin.

From this story we learn that true repentance begins with godly sorrow, which leads to a confession or admission of sinful behavior. Who should we confess our sins to? It is important to confess our sins to the person we have sinned against. When a person first comes to Jesus, he must confess to Jesus his sins against God. Sometimes the Spirit leads us to find a person we have sinned against. We may need to confess to them our sins against them and ask them to forgive us. This leads to an important result of repentance, that is, a clear conscience before both God and men.

This lesson is **important** because it gives an example from Paul's ministry, of converts who demonstrated godly sorrow.

The **main truth** of this lesson is that godly sorrow leads to repentance of sin to God and sometimes to people too.

To **review** this lesson, answer the following questions:

1. When the people of Ephesus experienced Godly sorrow, what sin did they confess?
A. If you said, "The sin of sorcery," then you are correct.

2. What did the believers do with their written scrolls of sorcery after confessing their sins?
A. If you said that they publicly burned them, you are right.

3. What was the value of the scrolls of sorcery that the believers in Ephesus burned?
A. If you said that the books were worth the annual wages for 150 men, you answered   correctly.

Your **assignment** for this lesson is to review the list of six foundation doctrines at least ten times until you have memorized the list.

4 Repentance: Change of Thinking

For thousands of years people thought the earth was flat. They believed that if you traveled to its edge, you would fall off! In 330 BC the Greek philosopher Aristotle, provided evidence that the earth is actually round. It would take hundreds, and in some places thousands, of years before people would change their minds. They were slow to believe that the earth is actually a round sphere.

In a similar way repentance involves a change in the way a person thinks. Someone might say that they have repented. If, however, they continue to think, speak, and do the things they have always done, then they have not truly repented.

The apostle Paul was a very religious Jew. His name, in the Hebrew language, is Saul. He was born in the Roman city of Tarsus. Saul grew up in Jewish society and was raised to obey the Jewish law. He studied the Old Testament and eventually became a student of the most renowned Jewish lawyer of his time. That was a Pharisee named Gamaliel. The Pharisees were the Jewish lawyers of their day, who studied to become experts on Jewish law. The Law was based on the Old Testament books written by Moses. Pharisees claimed Moses as their source of authority in what they taught. Saul admits that he was the ultimate Pharisee, obeying every letter of the Jewish law. He was very passionate about what he believed. He was so passionate that after the death and resurrection of Jesus, he began to persecute all Christians. He believed that Christian Jews were disobeying the Jewish law and were teaching others to do so as well.

A great persecution came upon the Early Church. One of the Christian deacons, a righteous man name Stephen, was arrested and tried before the Jewish high

priest. He was found guilty on false charges. His accusers
dragged him out of the city and stoned him to death. The
men who participated in the stoning of Stephen took off
their outer robes and laid them at the feet of Saul. He kept
their robes safe as he watched in approval of their stoning of
Stephen (Acts 6:8-8:1).

Saul began to persecute the church in Jerusalem. He
would take temple guards with him to break into the homes
of Christians. He had them dragged away in chains. But his
zeal could not be satisfied with Jerusalem alone. He heard
that Christians had fled from Jerusalem and were now
preaching Jesus in Damascus. Saul then went to the high
priest and obtained letters addressed to the Jewish
synagogues in Damascus. The letters gave him authority to
arrest Christians—whether men or women—and bring them
back to Jerusalem as prisoners.

Gathering a small band of temple guards, Saul set
out on the long trip to Damascus. It would take him four to
six days of travel to get there. We might imagine Saul's
thoughts as he approached Damascus. We can assume he
was making plans to meet with the various Jewish leaders
and to find the names of all those who had become
Christians.

Saul and his entourage were almost to Damascus
when something extraordinary happened. A brilliant flash of
light surrounded him and he bowed to the ground. Then a
voice began to call out to him, "Saul! Saul! Why do you
persecute me?"

Saul was shocked and afraid. "Who are you, Lord?"
Saul asked.

"I am Jesus, whom you are persecuting," the voice
replied. "Now get up and go into the city and you will be

told what you must do." And with that the light disappeared and Saul was alone. The men traveling with Saul stood there speechless. They had heard the sound, but did not see anyone. Saul got up from the ground, but when he opened his eyes he could see nothing. So, they led him by the hand into Damascus. For three days Saul did not eat or drink anything. He was still blind and very confused. Can you imagine the thoughts going through his mind? Everything that he had ever believed had been challenged. The persecution of the followers of Jesus had been the very focus of his zeal for God. But this Jesus had called to him from blinding light. This Jesus who was supposed to be a mere man and who had been crucified and buried was not dead, but alive! This risen Christ had appeared to him in a supernatural way! How could this be?

Unknown to Paul a disciple of Jesus, named Ananias, was living nearby. He was about to have his own encounter with the Lord. "Ananias!" The Lord said to him in a vision.

"Yes, Lord," he answered.

The Lord commanded him, "Go to the house of Judas on Straight Street and ask for a man from Tarsus named Saul, for he is praying. In a vision he has seen a man named Ananias come and place his hands on him to restore his sight."

"Lord!" Ananias answered in fear. "I have heard many reports about this man and all the harm he has done to your holy people in Jerusalem. And he has come here with authority from the chief priests to arrest all who call on your name!"

But the Lord said, "Go! This man is my chosen instrument to proclaim my name to the Gentiles and their kings and to the people of Israel."

And so, Ananias, with great fear, went to the house where Saul was staying. Placing his hands-on Saul, he said, "Brother Saul, the Lord Jesus, who appeared to you on the road as you came here, has sent me so that you may see again and be filled with the Holy Spirit." Immediately something like scales fell from Saul's eyes and he could see again.
Saul stood to his feet and was baptized as a Christian. He immediately began to preach in the synagogues of Damascus that Jesus is the Son of God (Acts 9:1-20).

This is an amazing story of the transforming power of Jesus in the lives of men. Saul, who was convinced that he was being zealous for God by persecuting Christians, had a complete change of mind and heart. He went from being a persecutor to becoming a proclaimer.

True repentance will result in a change of thinking. The change in thinking will result in a change of behavior. This is a very important concept. Some Christians try to have new believers follow a list of rules. This is not true repentance. Our lives and behaviors change, not because we have a new list of dos and don'ts but because our hearts and minds have been changed.

True repentance will always include a change of thinking. We have also learned in previous lessons that Godly sorrow leads to repentance and that repentance involves confessing our sins to God.

This lesson is **important** because it teaches that true repentance will always include a change of thinking, not just a new set of rules to follow.

The **main truth** of this lesson is that it is the Holy Spirit that leads a person to repentance—feeling godly sorrow, confessing their sins, and changing both their thinking and behavior.

Let us **review** this lesson with the following questions:

1. What happens to the way we think when we truly repent?
       A. If you said that repentance includes a change in the way we think, then you are correct.

2. What did the apostle Paul do to the church before he became a Christian?
       A. If you said that he persecuted the church, you are correct.

3. What happened to the apostle Paul on his way to Damascus?
       A. If you said, "Jesus appeared to Paul in a blinding light," you answered correctly.

Your **assignment** for this lesson is to watch this lesson at least three times until you are able to accurately tell the story of the apostle Paul on the road to Damascus. Then, find someone and tell the story to them. Discuss how important it is to have a change in thinking when you repent.

5 Repentance: Change in Direction

Have you ever been on a journey and found yourself lost? It is easy to do. Sometimes the directions you were given were inaccurate. Other times you misread the landmarks. Whatever the cause, when we become lost, we have to get back on the right path to get to our destination. There was a man on a journey who made a wrong turn and found himself on the wrong road, going the wrong direction. Rather than turning around and retracing his steps, he thought that he would just turn onto the next road. Maybe it would get him where he needed to go. Again, and again he turned onto a different road, hoping it was the right way. Soon he was very far from his destination and thoroughly lost.

In many ways our lives are like this man's journey. Until we know God, we are actually traveling away from him. We try so many paths, hoping to find peace, but none of them leads us to God. When we repent, we stop traveling away from God and turn around. Then we begin our journey anew, this time traveling towards God. Repentance requires a change in the direction of our lives. Many of the things we did before, we will no longer do. The disciple Matthew recorded Jesus' teaching on the road of life. Jesus said, "Enter through the narrow gate. For wide is the gate and broad is the road that leads to destruction, and many enter through it. But small is the gate and narrow the road that leads to life, and only a few find it" (Matt 7:13-14).

Jesus told a story about a man who had two sons. He was a man of wealth who had much livestock. He also had lands that had been handed down from father to son for many generations. Now the younger son came to his father with a request. He was tired of living in a small village and working hard. He wanted his inheritance now. This was an unheard-of request. The young son was insulting his father.

It would be as if he were saying that he wished his father was dead! The elder brother became angry. By asking the father for his share of the inheritance, the younger brother was causing part of the family land to be sold and some of the flocks to be sold too.

But the father loved his sons. He would not force them to obey his will. He would allow them to make their own choices, even if those choices brought about great sorrow. So, the father gave his younger son his share of the family estate.

The young man wasted no time in gathering his wealth and leaving the small rural village of his family. He traveled away from his father and family to a distant land, arriving as a stranger in a large city. It was obvious that he was from the country. His clothes and manners gave him away. But he did have wealth. Soon he was spending his inheritance on all of the pleasures the big city had to offer. His old clothes were replaced with new clothes that were more in keeping with a man of his wealth. He was surrounded by everything new, including foreign gods in temples that no Jewish man should enter.

The young man-made friends with other young men of the city. They were more than willing to help him spend his money on the violent entertainment there. But money that is spent on wine, rich foods, fine clothing, and immoral friends soon runs out. The day came when the young man had spent his entire inheritance. His money was gone and all of his friends were gone too. Alone, and without money, the young man found himself in trouble. Soon he had nothing left but the clothes on his back.

And then the land went into a time of famine. His stomach rumbling with hunger, he went to one of the farmers in the land. He was given a job feeding pigs. Can you imagine this young man's despair? He was a Jew. The Jewish law taught that pigs were unclean animals. No Jew would own pigs, let alone touch them. But the young man had reached the very bottom.

He was so hungry he wanted to eat the food that the pigs were eating. As he fed the pigs, his mind wandered back to his father's home. All of his father's servants had plenty of food to eat. And in that moment the young man made a decision. His life was going in the wrong direction. All of the things he thought he wanted, had not satisfied him, but had led him farther and farther away from his father. He made his decision. He was going to turn around and go back to his father. And so, he began the long journey home.

How the father had grieved for his lost son! Each day he kept watch, hoping that his son would return to him. Can you imagine how angry the people of the village were when the young man came home? He had not only rejected his father, but had rejected them as well! But the father saw his son a long way off and ran to him. This was an embarrassing thing to do. He was a man of importance in the village and people of his status and age just did not run!

The father's love for his son was so great that he was willing to embarrass himself and turn his son's shame upon himself. The young man cried out to his father and said, "Father, I am not worthy to be called your son!"

But the father embraced his son with deep love. He called to his servants to get a new robe for his son and to place a ring upon his finger and sandals on his feet. He then commanded that a great celebration be held. The fattened calf was to be killed and prepared for the party. Everyone in the village would be invited, for his son who was lost had come home.

This story wonderfully illustrates what we have learned about repentance. The boy first experienced godly sorrow while feeding the pigs. This led to a change in his thinking. He finally understood that everything he had done was empty and vain. Next, he did something about it. He changed his direction. He turned around and headed home towards his father. Finally, the young man confessed to his father his failure. And what was the result of his repentance? The father welcomed home his wayward son with open arms.

We have now learned four important aspects of repentance. First, Godly sorrow leads to true repentance. When we repent, we should confess our sins to God. Repentance always leads to a change in the way we think and a change in our direction. We no longer are going away from God, but now are on the narrow path that leads us ever closer to him.

This lesson is **important** because it uses one of Jesus' stories to teach that true repentance leads to a change in one's direction.

The **main truth** of this lesson is that God the Father welcomes with open arms those who truly repent.

To **review** this lesson, answer the following questions:

1. What kind of sorrow leads to repentance?
    A. If you said, "Godly sorrow," then you are correct.

2. What are the two changes that happen when we repent?
    A. If you said that we have a change of thinking and a change of direction, you are correct.

3. Who should we confess our sins to?

      A. If you said that we should confess our sins to God and confess our sins against a person to that person as well, you are right.

Your **assignment** for this lesson is to watch this lesson at least three times until you thoroughly understand the parable of the lost son and can tell the story. Then, find someone else and use the story to explain to them the four steps of true repentance towards God.

6 Repentance: Restitution

His wife did not want him smoking in the apartment, so he went outside and stood on his balcony. He had almost completed smoking a cigarette, when his wife called to him from inside. Without a thought, he threw the cigarette butt off the balcony and went in. After all, he was on the fourth floor, what harm could it cause? The cigarette butt, still smoldering, drifted down and landed on a stack of paper on the balcony of apartment 104. First there was smoke, and then there was fire. Soon the fire spread to the apartments around it. The fire would gut Tower 4 of the Al Baker apartment complex, leaving 120 families homeless. The man never thought that his careless act of throwing a cigarette off of his balcony would hurt anyone.

This is so typical of sinful behavior. People seldom think about how their sins can impact those around them. But sin not only affects the person who is sinning; it often affects others. We have discussed how repentance begins with Godly sorrow, which leads to confessing our sins to God. Sometimes when we have offended others, we should confess to them also and ask their forgiveness. In some situations, repentance will lead to restitution.

The Romans conquered the land of Israel 100 years before Jesus was born. They set a provincial government to rule over it. This led to heavy taxes being placed upon the people. There were taxes on almost everything and thus Rome required many tax collectors. Now the tax collectors were not government officials. They were actually small businessmen who had to purchase the right to collect taxes at a government auction. They did this by prepaying to Rome the taxes they were to collect. Rome would pay them interest on the prepayment of taxes. But they would have to work hard to collect the taxes due, in order to recover their investment and make a profit. The tax collectors were called publicans and, as you might imagine, were hated by the general population. Sometimes a person could not pay their taxes. So, the publican would loan them the money to cover the taxes, but at a high rate of interest. It was a common practice to cheat and overcharge people.

One day Jesus was on a trip that would cause him to pass through the ancient city of Jericho. The towering walls of Jericho had not protected its original inhabitants from being conquered hundreds of years earlier. Joshua and the people of Israel had marched around the walls for seven days. On the seventh day they marched around Jericho seven times. Then, with the blowing of rams' horns and shouts from the people, God caused the walls of Jericho to fall! Its people had been conquered.

Jesus' arrival in Jericho caused quite a stir. Not only were his 12 disciples with him, a crowd had gathered. They wanted to see the man who had healed the sick and fed the hungry. Living in Jericho was a wealthy tax collector named Zacchaeus. He also wanted to get a look at Jesus, but he was very short and could not see over the crowd. But Zacchaeus was used to getting what he wanted, so he ran ahead of the procession and climbed up into a sycamore-fig tree. Soon Jesus and the procession were passing in front of him. His view from the tree allowed him to see Jesus clearly. But it also allowed Jesus to see him as well. To his surprise, Jesus stopped right in front of him and then spoke. "Zacchaeus, come down from the tree immediately. I must stay at your house today." A murmur quickly spread through the crowd. Why was Jesus speaking to this man? Didn't Jesus know that Zacchaeus was a publican, a hated tax collector? Everyone knew that publicans cheated and stole from the people. They were considered the lowest of the low and chief among all sinners.

Zacchaeus climbed down from the tree and pushed through the crowd to stand before Jesus. He was overwhelmed that the Master would stop to speak to him. He knew what people thought of him. He also knew that the Master was incurring great shame by being willing to go to his home. Soon Jesus, his disciples, and Zacchaeus were at his home eating a meal together. People stood around and listened to Jesus teach. Zacchaeus felt the Holy Spirit convicting him of his sin. He wanted to become a follower of this man Jesus. "Look, Lord!" Zacchaeus said. "Here and now I give half of my possessions to the poor, and if I have cheated anybody out of anything, I will pay back four times the amount."

Jesus then answered him, speaking to everyone present, "Today salvation has come to this house, because this man, too, is a son of Abraham. For the Son of Man came to seek and to save the lost" (Luke 19:1-10).

Zacchaeus experienced something very dramatic that day. He was so moved that he was willing to give a great sum of money to the poor. He also vowed to make restitution for any harm he had caused. What could make a man do such a thing? We can imagine what might have been going through his mind while Jesus spoke. Surely, he felt godly sorrow. Along with this was the desire to confess and repent. But he was a man of action and his desire for repentance had to be demonstrated by his action. He would give half of his wealth to the poor and make restitution for any sins he had committed against others by cheating them.

Part of the repentance process is to make restitution when possible. For some sins, restitution is impossible. But, when it is within our power to do so, restitution is a powerful part of repentance. Do not be deceived into thinking that restitution is what causes our sins to be forgiven. Forgiveness comes to us through Jesus' death upon the cross. He has paid for our sins and it is only through making Jesus our Lord and Savior that we are saved and forgiven. But restitution accomplishes two distinct things. First it helps restore our relationships with those we have offended. Secondly, restitution is a powerful witness to everyone that God has done something amazing in our lives.

This lesson is **important** because it uses the story of Zaccheus to illustrate that true repentance often includes making restitution for wrongs committed.

The **main truth** of this lesson is that although forgiveness comes through Jesus, restitution, as a part of repentance, helps restore one's relationships with people and serves as a witness to God's transforming power in a life.

Let's **review** this lesson:

1. What was Zaccheus' profession?

A. If you said, "Zaccheus was a tax collector," you are correct.

2. Restitution can be an important part of repentance. How did Zaccheus demonstrate restitution?

A. If you said that Zaccheus said that he would pay back four times any money that he had cheated people out of, then you are right.

3. List the five aspects of repentance.

A. If you said, "Godly sorrow, a change of heart and direction, confession, and restitution," then you answered correctly.

Your **assignment** for this lesson is to watch this lesson at least three times. Then find someone and teach them about repentance, by telling them the story of Zaccheus.

7 Faith: Believing God

In our previous 5 lessons we have learned aspects of repentance which include: godly sorrow, a change of mind and direction, confession, and restitution. Today we will begin to learn about the second foundational doctrine, "Faith."

What is faith? "To believe" is the simple answer. Each night when we close our eyes to go to sleep, we fully believe and expect to awake the next morning. This confidence in what we believe is "faith." The New Testament writer of the Book of Hebrews wrote a much deeper definition of faith. He wrote that "faith is confidence in what we hope for and assurance about what we do not see" (Heb 11:1).

There were three young Jewish men that illustrate this definition of faith. They had a belief in God that would allow them to face certain death. By faith Moses led the Jewish people out of Egypt and into the land of Canaan. For 400 years the people would be led by various judges. Eventually the people demanded a king to rule over them, so God gave them kings. Some of the kings were godly men. Others led the people into idolatry. Israel reached its greatest power and wealth during the time of King David's son, Solomon. But Solomon's son was not a wise king like his father. During his reign the kingdom was split into two. The tribes of Benjamin and Judah formed the southern kingdom of Judah, and the ten northern tribes became Israel.

Now many of the kings of Judah were godly men, but most of the kings of Israel were not. When the people turned their hearts away from God, he allowed the nations around them to attack them. Finally, around 750 years before Jesus was born, the Assyrians conquered Israel. They carried the ten northern tribes into captivity. The Assyrians conquered much of modern Syria and Iraq, plus parts of southern Turkey too. God spared the people of Judah from Assyria. But 200 years later, the next major empire of the Middle East, the Babylonians, invaded Judah and conquered the land. Many conquerors during ancient times would kill all of the leaders of their conquered enemies. But the Babylonian king, Nebuchadnezzar, was different. He made his kingdom great by absorbing the best and brightest men of the lands he conquered into his own government. When Nebuchadnezzar conquered Judah he took back to his capital city many of the most educated young men in Israel. Among them were three young men whom he called Shadrach, Meshach, and Abednego. They would continue their education with the elite of Babylon.

King Nebuchadnezzar made an idol of gold that was 28 meters high and nearly three meters wide. He set the golden idol on the broad plain near his capital city of Babylon. He then invited all of his government leaders to its dedication. A great number of people gathered, including Shadrach, Meshach, and Abednego.

The herald loudly proclaimed to everyone present, "Nations and peoples of every language, this is what you are commanded to do: As soon as you hear the music sound, you must fall down and worship the image of gold that King Nebuchadnezzar has set up. Whoever does not fall down and worship, will immediately be thrown into a blazing furnace!"

Now Shadrach, Meshach and Abednego looked at each other in shock and fear. They were righteous Jewish men and knew that the Ten Commandments forbade worshipping any idol or foreign god. Each of them wrestled in their hearts about what they would do when the music sounded. Suddenly the music began. Across the plain the leaders of Babylon began to kneel and bow before the king's idol. Finally, everyone lay prostrate before the idol except for Shadrach, Meshach, and Abednego.

Word of this was brought to King Nebuchadnezzar and the three Jewish lads were dragged into his presence. "Is it true, Shadrach, Meshach, and Abednego, that you do not serve my gods or worship the image of gold I have set up?" the king yelled, furious with anger. "If you are willing to fall down and worship my idol when the music sounds, then I will spare your lives. But, if you continue to refuse to obey my command and worship my gods, then you will be thrown alive into the furnace of fire!"

Nervously the boys stood before the enraged king. Their hearts were filled with fear and dread. But they believed in their God. They believed that the God of the Israelites was the only true God.

"Well?" the king demanded. "What do you say?"

"King Nebuchadnezzar, we do not need to defend ourselves before you in this matter. If we are thrown into the blazing furnace, the God we serve is able to deliver us from it, and he will deliver us from Your Majesty's hand. But even if he does not, we want you to know, Your Majesty, that we will not serve your gods or worship the idol of gold you have set up" (Dan 3:1-18).

Can you imagine how furious this answer must have made the king? He became so angry that he ordered the furnace to be heated to seven times its normal heat. All of the government officials gathered to watch the spectacle of the three boys being burned alive. The king's strongest soldiers bound Shadrach, Meshach, and Abednego with ropes and threw them into the blazing fire. The fire's heat was so intense that the flames lashed out of the fire and killed the soldiers that threw the boys into the fire.

The king looked around at all of his government officials. They would now all understand and believe that they had to obey him or they too would be dealt with harshly. Suddenly there was a gasp from the crowd and people began to point towards the fire. King Nebuchadnezzar spun around to see what they were staring at. The king squinted his eyes at the brilliance of the flames. Suddenly, there in the midst of the fire he saw movement. It looked like there were people walking about in the fire. "Were there not only three men that were tied up and thrown into the fire?" the king asked.

"Certainly, Your Majesty." they replied in fear and amazement.

"Look, I see four men walking around in the fire, unbound and unharmed, and the fourth looks like a son of the gods!" The king spoke in awe. Then raising his voice, he called into the fire, "Shadrach, Meshach, and Abednego, servants of the Most High God, come out! Come here to me!"

So, Shadrach, Meshach and Abednego came out of the fire, and all of the government officials crowded around them in amazement. They reached out and touched their clothing and leaned close to them to detect any odor of smoke. But the three Jewish boys were not harmed in any way. Not a single hair of their heads was singed. Nor were their garments scorched by the flames. Only the ropes that had bound them were burned and gone.

Then King Nebuchadnezzar raised his voice and said, "Praise be to the god of Shadrach, Meshach and Abednego, who has sent his angel and rescued his servants! They trusted in him and defied my command. They were willing to give up their lives, rather than serve or worship any god except their own God. Therefore, I decree that the people of any nation or language who say anything against the God of Shadrach, Meshach, and Abednego be cut into pieces and their houses be turned into piles of rubble, for no other god can save in this way!" (Dan 3:19-29).

In this story we have a powerful example of faith towards God. The three boys believed that God could and would save them. Their faith or belief was so complete, that even if God did not deliver them, they would still trust in him.

This story is **important** because it teaches us that our faith is in God and his will, whether or not he rescues us from our circumstances.

The **main truth** of this lesson is that faith means believing God, even when we cannot see the outcome.

Let's **review** this lesson:

1. What is a simple definition for faith?
        A. If you said that to have faith is "to believe," you are right.

2. Shadrach, Meshach, and Abednego refused to do what?
        A. If you said that they refused to bow and worship the king's idol, then you are correct.

3. What happened when Shadrach, Meshach, and Abednego were thrown into the king's furnace of fire?
        A. If you said, "God honored their faith and delivered them alive," then you answered correctly.

Your **assignment** for this lesson is find someone and tell them the story of Shadrach, Meshach, and Abednego. Explain to them what it means to have faith.

8 Faith Pleases God

Raising children is an adventure. Sometimes we, as parents, are pleased and sometimes we are displeased. At times our children make us laugh with joy; other times we cry with frustration. One thing every child does is to ask their parents for things. We sometimes overlook the marvelous truth behind this. In order for a child to ask something of us, he must believe that we are able to meet his request. The request is actually an act of faith. The author of the Book of Hebrews wrote, "Without faith it is impossible to please God, because anyone who comes to him must believe that he exists and that he rewards those who earnestly seek him" (Heb 11:6).

The disciple Matthew wrote this story about Jesus meeting a man of great faith. Jesus and his disciples were traveling through the region of Galilee and entered the city of Capernaum. The fishing village was on the northwest coast of the Sea of Galilee and would become the base of operations for Jesus' ministry in Galilee.

When Jesus entered the city, a Roman centurion approached him and asked for help. Now Roman centurions were men of substantial authority. They were officers in the Roman army and commanded 100 to 200 men. Each centurion derived his authority from the officers above him and ultimately, from Caesar himself. The centurion was the officer that carried out the commands of Rome. Many centurions became men of great wealth and influence. And so, it was with the centurion that came out to meet Jesus upon his arrival in Capernaum. "Lord," the centurion said, "my servant lies at home paralyzed, suffering terribly."

This statement caught Jesus' attention. This military leader was coming to Jesus, not for his own need, but for that of a servant. It was not uncommon for masters to treat their servants cruelly. But some masters developed close friendships with their servants. Perhaps Jesus sensed that in the centurion's voice. "Shall I come and heal him?" Jesus asked.

"Lord, I do not deserve to have you come under my roof," the centurion humbly said. He treated Jesus with great honor and respect. "But just say the word, and my servant will be healed. For I myself am a man under authority, with soldiers under me. I tell this one, 'Go,' and he goes; and that one 'Come,' and he comes. I say to my servant, 'Do this,' and he does it."

When Jesus heard this he was amazed. This Roman soldier truly understood how authority worked and he was demonstrating his faith in Jesus' authority. Just as he had only to give the command for his men to obey, he believed that Jesus had only to give the command and his servant would be healed.

Jesus turned to all of those around him and said, "Truly I tell you, I have not found anyone in Israel with such great faith. I say to you that many will come from the east and the west, and will take their places at the feast with Abraham, Isaac and Jacob in the kingdom of heaven. But the subjects of the kingdom will be thrown outside, into the darkness, where there will be weeping and gnashing of teeth."

Then Jesus turned to the centurion and said, "Go! Let it be done just as you believed it would." And his servant was healed at that very moment (Matt 8:5-13).

From this incident in Jesus' life we learn a lot about faith and how important faith is to God. We see how the centurion's faith was rewarded. We also see how faith is linked to having a right relationship with God. Jesus taught that it would be through faith that people from around the world would become part of the kingdom of God. Those who thought they were Christians, but who did not have faith, would never enter into God's Kingdom. Indeed, as it is written in the Bible, "Without faith it is impossible to please God."

This story is **important** because it teaches that praying is demonstrating faith that God, our Father, will hear and answer us.

The **main truth** of this lesson is that God is pleased by the faith of anyone who comes to him, believing that he exists. He rewards those who seek him by giving them eternal life with him.

To **review** this lesson, answer the following questions:
1. What was a Roman centurion?
	A. If you said that a Roman centurion was an officer in the Roman army who commanded at least 100 soldiers, you are right.

2. What did the centurion want Jesus to do?
	A. If you said that the centurion wanted Jesus to heal his beloved servant, then you are correct.

3. What did Jesus say about the centurion's faith?
	A. If you answered, "Jesus said that he had not seen such great faith in all of Israel," then you answered correctly.

Your **assignment** is to memorize this simple verse from the Bible, "Without faith it is impossible to please God," Hebrews chapter 11, verse 6.

9 Faith Produces Miracles

Many things happen in life that cannot be separated from each other. For instance, you will not have rain unless there are clouds in the sky. Without a seed, a plant will not grow. Without faith, there cannot be a miracle. Two stories in the life of Jesus show this connection between faith and miracles.

Jesus' disciple Matthew wrote the first story in his Gospel. It all began when Jesus took Peter, James, and John with him to the top of a high mountain. He and his disciples had been ministering in a city called Caesarea Philippi. This city was about 40 kilometers (24 miles) north of the Sea of Galilee. It sat at the base of one of the tallest mountains in the area, Mount Hermon. Jesus had just rebuked his disciples a few days earlier because of their lack of faith. He had reminded them how he had fed 5,000 people with just two fish and five loaves and then had fed 4,000 people with only seven loaves.

Now Jesus, Peter, James, and John climbed to the top of one of the high mountains in the Hermon mountain chain. There something remarkable happened. Jesus suddenly began to glow and shine. His face became as bright as the sun. His clothes shone with a bright light. Two men suddenly appeared and began to talk to Jesus. A bright cloud appeared above them and a voice thundered from the cloud saying, "This is my Son, whom I love; with him I am well pleased. Listen to him!"

When the three disciples heard this, they fell face down on the ground, terrified. But Jesus touched them saying, "Get up, don't be afraid." When they stood up Jesus was alone (Matt 17:1-8).

The three disciples walked back down the mountain with Jesus to rejoin the rest of the disciples. When they found them, they were in the middle of a crowd of people having a heated discussion. Standing in the middle of the crowd were a man and his son. When the man saw Jesus, he knelt and said, "Lord, have mercy on my son. He has seizures and is suffering greatly. He often falls into the fire or into the water. I brought him to your disciples, but they could not heal him" (Matt 17:14-16).

The disciples looked at one another, somewhat embarrassed. They all had ministered before in Jesus' name and had seen miracles take place. But on this occasion, nothing had happened. They were wrestling with their personal belief and understanding of who Jesus was. He had rebuked them a few days earlier about their lack of faith. Now they were about to receive another rebuke. "You unbelieving and perverse generation," Jesus said. "How long shall I stay with you? How long shall I put up with you? Bring the boy here to me." Then Jesus cast out the demonic spirit that had possessed the boy and he was healed instantly.

Later the disciples questioned Jesus in private asking him, "Why couldn't we drive the demonic spirit out of the boy?"

Jesus responded by saying, "Because you have so little faith." Then Jesus taught them the significance of faith. "Truly I tell you, if you have faith as small as a mustard seed, you can say to this mountain 'Move from here to there,' and it will move. Nothing will be impossible for you" (Matt 17:14-20). Faith is a trust in God's Word and his will. Jesus had already told the disciples to heal the sick and drive out demons (Matt 10:8).

From this story we learn the connection between the faith of a person and his or her ability to believe God for miracles. Matthew wrote another incident in the life of Jesus that teaches us the other side of faith and miracles. Not only does the person who is performing the miracle need to have faith, but those who are receiving the miracle must have faith as well.

Jesus came to his home town of Nazareth. It was where he had grown up and was well known by everyone in the village. As was his custom he went to the synagogue and began to teach. Now the people in the village knew that he had never had any formal training like the Pharisees. They were amazed at his teachings. "Where did this man get this wisdom and these miraculous powers?" they asked. "Isn't this the carpenter's son? Isn't his mother's name Mary, and aren't his brothers, James, Joseph, Simon and Judas? Aren't all his sisters with us? Where then did this man get all these things?"

Instead of believing in him, they all took offense at him. Jesus then said to them, "A prophet is honored everywhere except in his own town and in his own home." And Jesus did not do many miracles there in his home town because of their lack of faith (Matt 13:54-58).

This is an incredible truth. Jesus, the Son of God, was unable to perform miracles there. He had unlimited faith, but those to whom he was trying to minister lacked faith. Christ's power did not depend on man's faith. However, unbelief prevented many opportunities for miracles, because not many people came to him.

This lesson is **important** because it teaches that when there is faith, miracles happen. When there is a lack of faith, miracles do not happen.

The **main truth** of these stories is that it takes faith in God's power and prayer to see miracles happen. Both the one ministering and the one with a need must have faith. God has promised to respond to those who ask in faith.

Let's **review** what we have discovered in this lesson:

1. Why were Jesus' disciples unable to drive the demon out of the demon-possessed boy?

A. If you said that the disciples lacked faith, you answered correctly.

2. Why was Jesus unable to perform many miracles in his home town?

A. If you said that the people in his home town lacked faith, then you are correct.

3. What must be present for miracles to take place?

A. If you said that faith must be present for miracles to take place, then you are right.

Your **assignment** for this lesson is to watch this lesson at least three times until you can retell the two stories from Jesus' life. Spend time praying and asking God to increase your faith in him, so that miracles will accompany your ministry.

10 Saved by Faith

People in the world today practice many religions. Each religion requires followers to perform certain tasks to achieve either right standing with their deity or reach a desired state of being. The followers of Judaism must obey the laws in the Old Testament in order to be blessed by God. The followers of Islam must perform the five pillars of Islam to have any hope of right standing with Allah. Hinduism is a road or path to liberation. In Buddhism we find the eight-fold path for correct living with the goal of individual enlightenment. In all of these religions the works of the individual follower determine his or her own success.

Christianity is the one great exception. The Christian's right standing with God is not based upon the individual's works. Instead it is based upon the sacrificial death and resurrection of Jesus Christ. The apostle Paul made this statement in a letter he wrote to the church in Ephesus: "It is by grace you have been saved, through faith—and this not from yourselves, it is the gift of God—not by works, so that no one can boast" (Eph 2:8-9).

To us, salvation is free. We cannot buy it, work for it, travel a path to it, or achieve it. Salvation is a free gift from God that was purchased by the death of Jesus. There is only one requirement for receiving God's salvation. We must believe in the Lord Jesus. The apostle Paul made this important statement in a letter he wrote to the church in Rome. "If you declare with your mouth, 'Jesus is Lord,' and believe in your heart that God raised him from the dead, you will be saved. For it is with your heart that you believe and are justified, and it is with your mouth that you profess your faith and are saved" (Rom 10:9-10).

The apostle Paul and his ministry partner, Silas, were on a missionary trip to the land of Macedonia. It is located just north of Greece. They had reached the city of Philippi and were having some success in preaching the gospel. Each day Paul and Silas, along with some fellow believers, would go to a place of prayer. Nearby was a female slave who was demon possessed. Many thought she could predict the future. She met the disciples on their way to pray and began to follow them, shouting, "These men are servants of the Most High God, who are telling you the way to be saved" (Acts 16:16-17).

Each day as they went to pray, this woman would follow them, shouting as they walked. Finally, Paul became so annoyed with this that he turned around and said to the demonic spirit, "In the name of Jesus Christ I command you to come out of her!" At that very moment the spirit left her and she was free.

Now most people would rejoice that a person had been delivered from demonic possession. But the female slave's owners became very angry because she could no longer make money for them by foretelling things. Enraged, they grabbed Paul and Silas and dragged them before the city's magistrates. A big commotion took place as a crowd gathered and joined in the attack against them. The magistrates, trying to calm the mob, had Paul and Silas beaten with rods and thrown into prison. They commanded the jailer to guard them carefully. The jailer did not need any extra motivation for keeping a close watch over his prisoners. He understood that he would be held responsible if anyone escaped. He could be put into prison himself or put to death. So, the jailer placed Paul and Silas in the inner cell and fastened their feet in the stocks.

About midnight Paul and Silas were praying and singing hymns to God. The other prisoners were listening quietly. Suddenly there was a violent earthquake. The prison was shaken so violently that the prison doors swung open. Even the chains that held the prisoners came loose. The sleeping jailer was suddenly wide awake. When he opened his eyes and saw the prison doors open, he was afraid. He thought surely everyone had escaped. Staggering to his feet, he drew his sword. He decided it would be better to kill himself than to suffer at the hands of the magistrates and live the rest of his life in prison. As he prepared to thrust his sword through his own belly, he heard a voice calling to him from within the prison. "Don't harm yourself! We are all here!" Paul called out.

The jailer quickly called for a light and found Paul and Silas. He brought them out of the prison and into his quarters. "Sirs, what must I do to be saved?" he asked.

Isn't it interesting that the prison guard thought that he had to **do** something to be saved. But Paul's answer did not require any great deed, but rather simply asked him to believe. Paul told him: "Believe in the Lord Jesus, and you will be saved—you and your household." Then they spoke the Word of the Lord to him and to all the others in his house. The jailer took them and washed their wounds. Then immediately he and his entire household were baptized. They were filled with joy because they had come to believe in God (Acts 16:18-31).

This story is **important** because it demonstrates the powerful truth that salvation is a gift. The only requirement for a person to receive this gift is for them to believe, that is, to have faith.

The **main truth** of this lesson is that no amount of good works can earn a person's salvation. It is by grace we are saved, through faith.

Let's **review** what we have discovered in this lesson:

1. What is a Christian's right standing with God based on?

 A. If you said it is based upon the sacrificial death and resurrection of Jesus Christ, you answered correctly.

2. What were Paul and Silas doing in prison at midnight?

 A. If you answered, "They were praying and singing hymns to God," you are correct.

3. What was the one requirement for the jailer, in order that he might be saved?

 A. If you answered that he had to believe in the Lord Jesus to be saved, then you are right.

 Your **assignment** for this lesson is to watch this lesson at least three times until you can retell the story of Paul and Silas in prison. The statements of Paul in regard to salvation are crucial for every believer to memorize. Thus, an additional part of your assignment is to memorize this verse from the Bible: "For it is by grace you have been saved, through faith--and this not from yourselves, it is the gift of God—not by works, so that no one can boast" Ephesians chapter 2, verses 8 and 9.

11 Faith and Works

Once there was a small river that flooded during the rainy season. Two local men decided they would build a rope bridge across the river. These men had built rope bridges before and felt confident that they would not face any major problems. But they soon discovered that it would not be as easy as they had hoped. Although there were many trees along the river, they could not find a place where there was a large tree on both sides of the river across from each other. This forced them to make a decision. They would have to use one large tree, and on the opposite bank, a much smaller one. After many hours the two men completed their rope bridge between the two trees.

"I believe that we have made a good bridge," the first man said to the other. "I believe that you are right," the second man replied. "And I think that the small tree is more than adequate to hold a man's weight." The first man rubbed his beard as he stared at the small tree intently and said, "I agree. You can be the first person who walks across the bridge!" This led to a great argument as to who should be the first to cross the river. Although they both said that they believed the tree would hold, neither of them was willing to be the first to try it.

James, the half-brother of Christ, and writer of the Book of James, talks about this in the Bible. This is what he wrote:

What good is it, my brothers and sisters, if someone claims to have faith but has no deeds? Can such faith save them? Suppose a brother or a sister is without clothes and daily food. If one of you says to them, "Go in peace; keep warm and well fed," but does nothing about their physical needs, what good is it? In the same way, faith by itself, if it is not accompanied by action, is dead.

But someone will say, "You have faith; I have deeds."

Show me your faith without deeds, and I will show you my faith by my deeds. You believe that there is one God. Good! Even the demons believe that—and shudder.

You foolish person, do you want evidence that faith without deeds is useless? Was not our father Abraham considered righteous for what he did when he offered his son Isaac on the altar? You see that his faith and his actions were working together, and his faith was made complete by what he did. And the scripture was fulfilled that says, "Abraham believed God, and it was credited to him as righteousness," and he was called God's friend. You see that a person is considered righteous by what they do and not by faith alone.

In the same way, was not even Rahab the prostitute considered righteous for what she did when she gave lodging to the spies and sent them off in a different direction? As the body without the spirit is dead, so faith without deeds is dead (James 2:14-26).

James ends this passage with a powerful statement. He says that "faith without works is dead." According to a previous lesson, Paul taught us that we are saved by grace through faith. Paul makes it very clear that we cannot be saved by works or good deeds. We receive faith by believing, having faith in, Jesus Christ. James is not disagreeing with Paul. Rather, he is making the case that true faith will always produce works of faith. James tells the story of Abraham and his son Isaac.

God had promised Abraham that his descendants would inherit all the land of Israel. His wife gave birth to their son Isaac when she was 90 years old. God promised that it would be through Isaac that the promise would be fulfilled. One day God commanded Abraham to take his 13-year-old son, Isaac, to the top of the mountain to sacrifice him. So, Abraham took Isaac up to the top of the mountain. He prepared the wood for the sacrifice fire, bound his son Isaac, and place him upon the wood. He drew his knife and held it up, prepared to kill Isaac.

Suddenly, God called to Abraham and stopped him.

This is an amazing story of faith. Abraham's faith in God was so complete that he knew in his heart that God would not break his promise. He knew that God had said that it would be through Isaac that the inheritance would come. Therefore, if Abraham obeyed God and sacrificed Isaac, Abraham believed that God would even bring Isaac back from the dead to fulfill his promise (Heb 11:19).

This lesson is **important** because this story of Abraham and the teaching of the apostle James show us that true faith will always result in action—works of faith.

The **main truth** of this lesson is that though our good works do not save us, yet faith without works is dead. We need both.

Let's **review** what we have discovered in this lesson:
1. The Apostle James wrote that faith without works was what?
A. If you said that "faith without works is dead," you are correct.

2. Can a person be saved by doing good works?
A. If you said no, a person must be saved by faith, then you are correct.

3. What apostle said that faith and works are tied together?
A. If you said that the apostle James taught that faith and works are tied together, then you are correct.

12 Baptism: Water

In this course we are learning about the six foundation doctrines that every Christian should know. The author of the Book of Hebrews wrote this:
"Therefore leaving the elementary teaching about the Christ, let us press on to maturity, not laying again a foundation of repentance from dead works and of faith toward God, of instruction about washings and laying on of hands, and the resurrection of the dead and eternal judgment" (Heb 6:1-2). In this lesson we begin learning about the doctrine of washings or baptisms.

The Bible tells us a wonderful story about a man named John. The story begins with Zechariah, who was of the descendants of Aaron, the brother of Moses. The descendants of Aaron were the priests in Israel. Zechariah was married to Elizabeth. She was related to Mary, who would become the mother of Jesus.

Now Zechariah and Elizabeth had grown old. They had never had children, because she was unable to conceive. One day while Zechariah was performing the priestly duties in the temple, an angel appeared to him. The angel told him that his wife Elizabeth would become pregnant in her old age and that a son would be born to them. It happened exactly as the angel had predicted and Zechariah and Elizabeth had a son. They named him John.

John grew up and lived in the wilderness by the Jordan River, not far from Jerusalem. He wore simple clothes made of camel hair and ate locusts and wild honey. John became a prophet in the land of Israel. He went about proclaiming, "Repent, for the kingdom of heaven has come near" (Matt 3:2). Everyone marveled at his message and many argued as to who he was—a madman or a prophet. But the Bible goes on to say that John was the one spoken of through the prophet Isaiah: "A voice of one calling in the wilderness, 'Prepare the way for the Lord, make straight paths for him.'"

People came to him from Jerusalem and all of Judea, confessing their sins. John baptized them in the Jordan River. The baptism was a sign of a person humbling himself and recognition of the person's repentance. Even some of the Jewish leaders came out to see John. Their interest was not so much in repentance, but in finding out who this man was and what he was teaching. John warned them that true repentance would produce righteous deeds. He then said, "I baptize you with water for repentance. But after me comes one who is more powerful than I, whose sandals I am not worthy to carry. He will baptize you with the Holy Spirit and fire" (Matt 3:11).

Jesus himself would be baptized by John. Now John recognized Jesus as the Son of God and at first refused to baptize him saying, "I need to be baptized by you!" But Jesus replied to him, "Let it be so now; it is proper for us to do this to fulfill all righteousness" (Matt 3:15). Jesus did not need to repent, but he was willing to humble himself and be baptized. Some of John's disciples would leave him and become disciples of Jesus.

Baptism was to become a very important event in the ministry of the church. These are the final words of Jesus, given to his disciples, just before he ascended into heaven: "All authority in heaven and on earth has been given to me. Therefore, go and make disciples of all nations, baptizing them in the name of the Father and of the Son and of the Holy Spirit, and teaching them to obey everything I have commanded you. And surely, I am with you always, to the very end of the age" (Matt 28:18-20).

We have learned in previous lessons that salvation comes through faith and repentance. There is, however, a very important third step. Everyone who makes Jesus the Lord of their life should be baptized in the name of the Father, Son, and Holy Spirit. Baptism declares that the new believer has become a follower or disciple of Jesus. In baptism we follow Christ's example and identify with him.

The Bible tells the story of an Ethiopian official, who was riding along the road in his chariot. He was reading from the Old Testament prophet, Isaiah. Meanwhile Philip, one of the first deacons, was led by the Lord to go to that very road. There he met the Ethiopian in the chariot and said, "Do you understand what you are reading?"

"How can I," the Ethiopian said, "unless someone explains it to me?" So, Philip jumped up into the chariot and explained how the prophet Isaiah had predicted the life, ministry, and death of Jesus. As they rode along the road they came to a place where there was some water and the Ethiopian said, "Look, here is water. What can stand in the way of my being baptized?" Immediately they stopped and Philip baptized the Ethiopian official (Acts 8:26-38).

Many have asked if it is possible to be a Christian and not be baptized. Jesus said this, "Whoever has my commands and keeps them is the one who loves me. The one who loves me will be loved by my Father, and I too will love them and show myself to them" (John 14:21). It is the command of Jesus that everyone who would be his disciple should be baptized. Thus, every believer should be baptized. We saw this with the Ethiopian. As soon as he believed, he wanted to be baptized.

The world also recognizes the importance of water baptism. Most religions do not recognize that a person has become a Christian until they are baptized in water.

This story is **important** because it teaches that every person who becomes a follower of Jesus should be baptized in water.

The **main truth** of this lesson is that by being baptized in water, a believer follows Christ's example and his command. Through baptism a person testifies that he or she has become a Christian.

Let's **review** what we have discovered in this lesson:

1. In our lesson today we have learned that once a person comes to Christ, he should do what with water?
     A. If you said, "Be baptized," then you answered correctly.

2. In whose name should every believer be baptized?
     A. If you said that every believer should be baptized in the name of the Father, Son, and Holy Spirit, you are right.

3. Jesus had a relative named John who preached repentance and did what?
     A. If you said that John baptized in water people who repented, you are correct.

Your **assignment** for this lesson is to listen to the lesson at least three times until you understand the principle of baptism in water. Then find someone and discuss the importance of water baptism in the life of a believer.

13 Baptism: Holy Spirit

It was the dry season and the countryside had turned brown. Most vegetation had disappeared. Everywhere one looked it was brown and dry, except for a single line of green trees and bushes growing by the river. Water continued to flow in the river during the dry season. Where did the water come from? There was no lake at the head of the river feeding it during the dry season. The water had to be coming from somewhere. A closer examination of the slow-moving river revealed the source of its continual flow. There were places in the river where it bubbled and swirled, revealing that great underground springs were the source of the river's water. Powerful underground forces propelled the water upwards until it burst through the surface bringing the life-giving water to a dry and barren land.

In this lesson we will learn about a spiritual spring of living water. Each fall the Jewish people have a celebration called the Feast of Booths. This was an important festival that all Jews were required to attend. It came at the end of the harvest season. It was given to the Jews to help them remember how God had provided for them. During their 40-year pilgrimage to the land of Israel from Egypt, God had given them food, water, and shelter. It is called the Feast of Booths, because during the week-long celebration families would construct simple booths from branches. They lived in them and ate the feasts that were prepared for the festival (Lev 23:33-43).

In the Gospel written by the disciple John, we learn about Jesus going up to Jerusalem to celebrate the Feast of Booths. Jesus had been ministering in Galilee. News of his miracles had spread throughout the land. People were in constant conversation about him. Some called him a prophet of God. Others considered him to be a heretic. In the midst of the Feast week Jesus went up to the temple to teach. The Jewish temple was divided into courtyards. The large outer court was called the court of the Gentiles. Gentiles are anyone who is not a Jew. This large courtyard was the place where people from many nations came. The inner courtyards were restricted to Jews only. Any Gentile who entered the inner courts could be executed.

Jesus entered into the courtyard and began to teach. A crowd quickly gathered. They were astonished at his teaching saying, "How did this man get such learning, without having been taught?" Jesus, hearing their whisperings, replied. "My teaching is not my own. It comes from the one who sent me. Anyone who chooses to do the will of God will find out whether my teaching comes from God or whether I speak on my own" (John 7:15-17).

Now the Jewish leaders were jealous of Jesus and felt threatened by his teaching. They sought to arrest him. Jesus slipped away, only to return on the last day of the feast. He stood in the midst of the courtyard and proclaimed, "If anyone is thirsty, let him come to me and drink. Whoever believes in me, as the Scripture has said, streams of living water will flow from his innermost being." The crowd listened in disbelief. What did Jesus mean by this statement? The disciple John said that Jesus was referring to the Baptism in the Holy Spirit (John 7:37-38).

After Jesus was raised from the dead, he appeared to his disciples over a period of 40 days. Finally, he gathered them together and commanded them not to leave Jerusalem. They were to wait there for what the Father had promised. Then Jesus made his final statement before ascending into heaven. Jesus said, "But you will receive power when the Holy Spirit comes on you; and you will be my witnesses in Jerusalem, and in all Judea and Samaria, and to the remotest parts of the earth" (Acts 1:8).

The Baptism in the Holy Spirit is one of the most important aspects of the Christian life. When a person repents, the blood of Christ washes away all sins and the Holy Spirit enters a person. This is salvation. Baptism in the Holy Spirit should happen next in the new Christian's life. Whereas water baptism happens on a person's outside, the Baptism in the Holy Spirit happens on the inside. Jesus said that out of our innermost being will flow a river of living water. This river is the Holy Spirit welling up inside of us and pouring out of us.

The Baptism in the Holy Spirit often comes as a Christian is praying or worshipping God. The worshipper experiences spiritual pressure building within. It is like the underground pressure that pushes water from deep within the earth, until it finally bursts out as a spring. In the same way, a person feels a spiritual pressure building inside. This often evokes powerful emotions. Joy and praise and worship overwhelm you. You feel like you will burst if you don't speak. You suddenly hear yourself speaking to God in words you do not know or understand.

The apostle Paul describes this speaking in tongues by saying, "Likewise the Spirit helps us in our weakness; for we do not know how to pray as we ought, but the Spirit himself intercedes for us with groanings too deep for words" (Rom 8:26, RSV). Speaking in tongues is the outpouring or overflowing of the Holy Spirit from within the Christian. It is a baptism that does not happen on the outside. It starts on the inside and flows outward.

This story is **important** because it explains the teaching and instruction of Jesus about the Baptism in the Holy Spirit.

The **main truth** of this lesson is that any believer who is thirsty for more of Jesus, should pray to be baptized in the Holy Spirit. Not only will the person's thirst be satisfied, but the Spirit will flow from him or her and give them new power to witness. Others around them will be blessed.

Let us **review** what we have discovered in this lesson:

1. Today we have learned that Jesus taught about a river of living water flowing out of us. What is this river of living water?
A. If you said that the river of living water is the Holy Spirit, you answered correctly.

2. What is it called when the Holy Spirit wells up inside of a Christian and overflows out of them?
A. If you said that this is the Baptism in the Holy Spirit, you are right.

3. Should every Christian be baptized in the Holy Spirit?
A. If you said that Baptism in the Holy Spirit is very important for every Christian, you   are correct.

Your **assignment** for this lesson is to listen to it at least three times until you fully understand the teaching. If you have not yet received the Baptism in the Holy Spirit, spend time praying, worshipping, and asking Jesus to fill you.

14 Baptism: Speaking in Tongues

About 30 boys gathered in the middle of the football playing field. They stood in a line in front of two of the older boys. A football lay on the ground in front of them. "I'll take the big kid." The first older boy said as they began choosing sides for a game of football. Among those wishing to be chosen was a small dark-skinned boy. Everyone there had brown skin, dark hair, and dark brown eyes. But it was obvious that this one boy was not from their village, or for that matter, even their country.

One by one the two captains chose their teams. It was obvious that neither captain was going to take a chance on a small kid, whom they did not know. As far as they were concerned, he probably knew nothing about playing football. Both teams were almost complete when suddenly the small dark-skinned boy stepped forward and picked up the football. Suddenly everyone began to laugh. "What are you going to do with that?" they teased.

The boy slowly turned to face one of the goals. It was 45 meters away! Then, he dropped the ball. It bounced once and in one smooth, powerful movement, the boy kicked the ball towards the goal. The ball flew through the air with a vicious side spin, curving dramatically as it entered the net in the upper corner. All of the boys just stood there in shock. Then, one of the captains said, "I'll take the small kid!"

An old English saying goes like this, "Seeing is believing." Remember Thomas, one of Jesus' disciples? He expressed a similar view when he heard that Jesus had risen from the dead. He would not believe it until he saw Jesus himself.

The apostle Peter had an experience similar to this. It was after Jesus had ascended into heaven and the believers in Jerusalem had been baptized in the Holy Spirit. That had been a miraculous day! The power of God had swept through the upper room where they had gathered to pray. Every one of them had been filled with the Holy Spirit and had begun to speak in tongues. Peter and all of the other believers were Jews. They knew that Jesus was the Messiah that had been promised to their people. Jesus had taught them that God loved the entire world. They did not yet really understand, however, that salvation was for everyone, not just Jews. Three amazing events happened that brought Peter and the entire Christian community the truth that Jesus and his Gospel were for all mankind.

In the city of Caesarea lived a Roman captain named Cornelius. He loved God very much. But neither he, nor anyone in his household, knew about Jesus. One afternoon something amazing happened to him. An angel appeared to him and told him to send for Simon Peter. You can imagine how surprised Cornelius must have been. But he obeyed and sent two servants to find Peter in Joppa.

Meanwhile, Peter was experiencing the second amazing event. He was having a vision! In the vision God challenged his Jewish traditions. Jews are commanded to be a separated people and not to enter into a home that did not belong to a fellow Jew. To associate with anyone who was not a Jew would cause them to become ceremonially dirty and unclean. It was just after this vision that the men arrived from Cornelius. Now Peter, being a good Jew, would never consider going to a non-Jew's house. But with the vision fresh in his mind, Peter and a few fellow believers, set off with the men to go to the house of Cornelius.

Cornelius humbly greeted Peter when he arrived and told him about the angel that had visited him. Peter then began to preach to Cornelius, his relatives, friends, and servants who had all gathered in his home. "I now realize how true it is that God does not show favoritism but accepts from every nation the one who fears him and does what is right. You know the message God sent to the people of Israel, announcing the good news of peace through Jesus Christ, who is Lord of all," Peter said as he began his message. He continued by telling them about Jesus' death on the cross and how God had raised him from the dead.

Now, while Peter was still preaching, the Holy Spirit fell upon Cornelius and all who were gathered in his house. Peter and his fellow believers watched and listened in amazement. They heard all of those present speaking in tongues and praising God (Acts 10:1-46). These were not Jews, yet God had filled them. They were baptized with the same Holy Spirit with the proof of speaking in tongues. It was the same way the 120 had received on the Day of Pentecost! Seeing was believing! It was clear that God had poured out his Spirit on these Gentiles. So Peter ordered that they also be baptized in water. He stayed with them a few days and taught them more about Jesus.

Jesus promised the gift of the Baptism in the Holy Spirit to every believer. The apostle Peter proclaimed this in his first sermon on the Day of Pentecost. "Repent and be baptized, every one of you, in the name of Jesus Christ for the forgiveness of your sins. And you will receive the gift of the Holy Spirit. The promise is for you and your children and for all who are far off—for all whom the Lord our God will call" (Acts 2:38-39).

This lesson is **important** because it explains how God clearly showed the disciples that salvation, baptism in water, and baptism in the Holy Spirit are for all people.

The **main truth** of this story is that God has no favorites. Anyone who believes in Jesus as God's Son can be saved and baptized in water. And they will be baptized in the Holy Spirit with the evidence of speaking in tongues.

Let's **review** this lesson:
1. Peter was preaching to Cornelius and his entire household when they received what?

     A. If you answered that they received the Baptism in the Holy Spirit, then you answered correctly.

2. How did Peter and his friends know that Cornelius and his household had received the Baptism in the Holy Spirit?

     A. If you said that Cornelius and his entire household began to speak in tongues when   the Holy Spirit came upon them, you are correct.

3. Who did Peter say that the gift of the Holy Spirit is for?

     A. If you said that the promise of the Holy Spirit is for you, your children, and for all who are far off, you are right.

Your **assignment** for this lesson is to listen to it at least three times until you can tell the story of Peter and the house of Cornelius. Gather a group of believers and tell them the story. Then pray together, asking for God to fill everyone present with his Holy Spirit.

15 Baptism: The Power to Witness

What makes a man brave? Is it possible for a man who acts cowardly to become brave? It is very hard for a person to stand up against forces that seem overwhelming. But when that person has access to something very powerful, they suddenly are not fearful, but are confident. In this lesson you will learn that the Baptism in the Holy Spirit gives supernatural power to the one baptized. This power was promised to us by Jesus. And it is given to us for a very special purpose.

Just before Jesus ascended into heaven, he spoke to his disciples and said this; "You will receive power when the Holy Spirit comes on you; and you will be my witnesses in Jerusalem, and in all Judea and Samaria, and even to the remotest parts of the earth" (Acts 1:8). The promise of power to the believer comes through the Baptism in the Holy Spirit. The purpose of the power is to be a witness at home, across your nation, and even to the rest of the world.

Peter was a fisherman and one of Jesus' first disciples. He was not highly educated and had a rash impulsive personality. Of all of the disciples, Peter was the one who was quick to offer an opinion. Sometimes he got it right; often he got it wrong.

Now Jesus and the disciples had just completed celebrating the Passover meal. Judas had left to betray Jesus to the Jewish Priests. So, after singing a hymn, Jesus and the eleven left the upper room. They walked through the streets of Jerusalem as night fell. Jerusalem was not a large city by modern standards. With a population of perhaps 20- to 30,000 people, it would be considered a small city today. But Jerusalem was a walled city which held the most holy place in all of Judaism, the temple of God. So, the disciples slipped out of the city through one of the gates located in the eastern wall. Before them rose a small mountain-ridge covered with olive groves, rightly called the Mount of Olives.

As they walked, Jesus shocked them with a prophetic statement. "This very night you will all fall away because of me, for it is written: 'I will strike the shepherd, and the sheep of the flock will be scattered'" (Matt 26:31). All of the disciples knew that he was the shepherd and they the sheep.

While the disciples grieved when they heard this, impetuous Peter had to boast of his bravery. Peter said, "Even if all fall away because of you, I never will."

Jesus looked at Peter with fondness and said, "Truly I tell you, this very night, before the rooster crows, you will disown me three times."

To this Peter again declared, "Even if I have to die with you, I will never disown you." And all the other disciples said the same (Matt 26:33-35).

Before the night was over, Jesus was arrested by a mob and all the disciples fled, including Peter. Jesus was led to the house of Caiaphas, the high priest, where all of the scribes and elders were gathered. Now while Jesus was inside suffering a mockery of a trial, Peter and John entered into the high priest's courtyard. A servant girl came up to Peter and said, "You also were with Jesus of Galilee." But Peter denied it.

Peter moved over to the courtyard's gateway only to be met with another servant girl, who also accused him of being with Jesus. Again, Peter denied it. A short time later a few others in the courtyard came up to Peter and said,

"Surely you are one of them; for even the way you talk gives you away."

Then Peter began to curse and swear, "I do not know the man!" Suddenly a rooster crowed. Peter realized he had done exactly as Jesus had said he would. He had denied Christ three times. Peter thought that he was so brave, and yet, deep inside he was cowardly. In deep embarrassment and shame, Peter went outside and wept bitterly (Matt 26:69-75).

Jesus was crucified, buried in a tomb, and raised back to life on the third day. He appeared to his disciples on many occasions. On the fortieth day, they all stood on the mountainside, as Jesus promised his disciples the power of the Holy Spirit. He then ascended into heaven. The disciples returned to Jerusalem to pray and wait for the gift that Christ had promised.

The disciples waited for ten days in prayer and expectation. They were all gathered together in the upper room of a building on the day of the Jewish festival, called Pentecost. This feast happened on the fiftieth day after Passover and was a time of great celebration as all Jews came to Jerusalem to celebrate the wheat harvest. Because of this the streets were packed with Jewish visitors from throughout the Roman Empire. It was early in the morning, just 9 a.m. Suddenly a tremendous rushing wind burst into the upper room. Everyone there was filled with the Holy Spirit and began to praise God in languages they did not know.

The noise was so great, that the people of Jerusalem came running to see what was happening. They stood around in shock as they heard God being praised in the languages of their home countries. Some said that the disciples were drunk. Others thought that they had gone mad. But something supernatural was happening! Peter, the coward who denied Christ three times, suddenly stepped forward. He was a changed man. Raising his voice, he began to preach under the powerful anointing of the Holy Spirit. He spoke not as a man full of fear, but as a man empowered with supernatural boldness. At the end of his sermon all the people were grieved because of their sins and cried out, "Brothers, what shall we do?"

Then Peter gave the first altar call in church history saying, "Repent, and be baptized, every one of you, in the name of Jesus Christ for the forgiveness of your sins. And you will receive the gift of the Holy Spirit. The promise is for you and your children and for all who are far off—for all whom the Lord our God will call" (Acts 2:37-39). And with that, 3,000 people became believers.

This is the story of two Peters, one a braggart and a coward, the other a bold preacher. What made the difference? The difference was exactly what Jesus promised before he ascended into heaven. "You will receive power when the Holy Spirit comes on you and you will be my witnesses in Jerusalem, and in all Judea and Samaria, and even to the remotest parts of the earth" (Acts 1:8).

This story is **important** because it teaches you just how much the Baptism of the Holy Spirit can change and empower those who are baptized. Like Peter, you can boldly proclaim God's truth to those around you, as the Holy Spirit gives you power.

The **main truth** of this story is that in our own strength we will fall short of becoming the witnesses to the world that God intended for us to be. We need the power of the Holy Spirit to anoint our words and help us overcome our weaknesses.

Let's **review** the main points of this lesson by answering these questions:

1. What was Peter really like before Jesus' death?
    A. If you said that Peter was a braggart and a coward, then you are correct.

2. What was Peter like after he received the Baptism in the Holy Spirit?
    A. If you said, "Peter became bold after the Holy Spirit came upon him," you are correct.

3. What did Jesus say the power of the Holy Spirit was for?
    A. If you said that the Holy Spirit would give them power to be witnesses, you are right.

Your **assignment** for this lesson is to pray and ask God to fill you with his Holy Spirit and to make you a bold witness for Christ. Memorize the words of Jesus to the disciples: "You will receive power when the Holy Spirit comes on you and you will be my witnesses in Jerusalem, and in all Judea and Samaria, and even to the remotest parts of the earth" (Acts 1:8). This is his promise to each of us today.

16 Baptism: Baptized in Fire

John the Baptist was preaching to people who had come to the Jordan River to be baptized. He made this most remarkable statement, "I baptize you with water for repentance, but he who is coming after me is mightier than I, whose sandals I am not worthy to carry. He will baptize you with the Holy Spirit and with fire" (Matt 3:11). In this statement, we discover three aspects of baptism. Water baptism is the recognition that a person has repented. The baptism in the Holy Spirit fills the believer with power and boldness. What does it mean to be baptized with fire? This lesson will help you learn what baptism with fire means.

A certain gold miner went to the mountain in search of gold. He would dig rocks and dirt out of the mountainside and then dump a shovelful into his large flat pan. Pouring water into the pan, he would begin to rock the pan gently back and forth. The water would carry all of the soil and small rocks away, leaving behind the much heavier flakes of gold. This gold has great value, but still requires one more step. It must be refined. So, the gold is then placed into a small ceramic pot called a crucible. It is heated to temperatures of almost 1100 degrees Celsius (2000 degrees Fahrenheit). The extreme fire and heat melt the gold and burns off all of the impurities, resulting in the gold becoming pure.

The apostle Peter wrote this in a letter to Jewish exiles: "In this you greatly rejoice, though now for a little while, you may have had to suffer grief in all kinds of trials. These have come so that the proven genuineness of your faith—of greater worth than gold, which perishes even though refined by fire—may result in praise, glory and honor when Jesus Christ is revealed" (1Peter 1:6-7). Peter understood that just like gold is refined by fire, so also our faith in Christ will be tested and refined through various trials. Becoming a Christian does not mean that all of life's difficulties and hardships will disappear.

One afternoon after the day of Pentecost, Peter and John were going up to the temple to pray. They came upon a man that was lame. He had been unable to walk since birth. Peter, being full of the Holy Spirit, reached down and took the man by the hand. As he helped him up, Peter commanded, "In the name of Jesus Christ of Nazareth, walk!" Immediately the man was healed and everyone around was amazed (Acts 3:1-10). Peter then preached a powerful sermon. As he was preaching the captain of the temple guard and some religious leaders seized both him and John. They dragged them off and threw them into jail.

It would be a long night for Peter and John. Being in prison and fearing what a judge might do to them would cause most men to become very humble and afraid. The next day, Peter and John were dragged out of jail and taken to stand before the most powerful religious leaders in all of Jerusalem. These men were not only religious leaders, but were empowered to be judges in religious matters. They were the very ones who had judged Jesus and sentenced him to death. It had been less than two months since Peter had stood outside in the courtyard of the high priest and had denied Jesus three times. Peter and John were in a very difficult situation. They now stood before men who had the power to destroy their lives.

"By what power or what name, did you do this?" They demanded an answer of Peter and John in regard to the miracle. How would Peter respond? Would he respond in fear? Would his faith fail him again? Would the fire of this trial burn his faith up or would it refine his faith?

Peter slowly turned to face his accusers and then said, "Rulers and elders of the people! If we are on trial today for an act of kindness shown to man who was lame and are being asked how he was healed, then know this, you and all the people of Israel: It is by the name of Jesus Christ of Nazareth, whom you crucified but whom God raised from the dead, that this man stands before you healed!" (Acts 4:1-10).

The elders were shocked and perplexed. No one ever talked to them in such a manner. They knew that Peter and John were uneducated fisherman and yet, here they stood with such confidence. They ordered that Peter and John be taken outside while they conferred with one another. After discussion, they reached a conclusion. It was obvious that a very noteworthy miracle had happened, but they wanted to stop the growth of Christianity. They decided that they would have to use the weight and authority of the priesthood to silence them. Peter and John were brought back into the council. "You are commanded not to teach or preach anymore in the name of Jesus," they insisted.

What would Peter do? Would this threat from the religious leaders overcome his faith? But Peter and John answered them, "Whether it is right in the sight of God to listen to you rather than to God, you must judge; for we cannot stop speaking about what we have seen and heard!" (Acts 4:19-20). And after being threatened again, Peter and John were released and returned to their fellow disciples. Peter and John's faith was tried by fire that day and they withstood the test.

The process of going through life's trials and tests is very important for the believer. Such difficult times are the refining fire that purifies our faith and draws us closer to God. The fire of temptation helps us discover the areas of our lives that need to be purified and strengthened. The fire of physical sicknesses and diseases helps us learn to depend upon Christ and not our own physical strength. The fire of business difficulties can purify our motives and integrity. The fire of strained and broken relationships can help us refine our character and allow us to be more Christlike.

The apostle Paul wrote this: "Who shall separate us from the love of Christ? Shall trouble or hardship or persecution or famine or nakedness or danger or sword? As it is written: 'For your sake we face death all day long; we are considered as sheep to be slaughtered.' No, in all these things we are more than conquerors through him who loved us. For I am convinced that neither death nor life, neither angels nor demons, neither the present nor the future, nor any powers, neither height nor depth, nor anything else in all creation, will be able to separate us from the love of God, that is in Christ Jesus our Lord" (Rom 8:35-39).

This lesson is **important** because it teaches clearly that God often allows trials and hardships in the life of a Christian. These are for the purpose of strengthening and refining their faith, as by fire, and making them more like Christ.

The **main truth** of this lesson is that though baptism by fire comes your way, nothing can separate you from God's love and power. If you continue to put your faith in Christ, the Holy Spirit will give you the victory over any temptation or difficulty.

Here are a few questions to **review** this lesson:

1. Why were Peter and John arrested?
      A. If you said that Peter and John were arrested because of the healing of a lame man, then you are correct.

2. When Peter and John were on trial for healing the lame man, what did the religious leaders command them to do?

A. If you said that they were commanded not to preach or teach in the name of Jesus, you are right.

3. What is the purpose of fire, that is, temptations and trials, in the Christian's life?
A. If you said that these things refine and strengthen our faith, then you are correct.

Your **assignment** for this lesson is find someone who is going through a difficult trial and encourage them with this story and with prayer.

17 Laying on of Hands: Imparting a Blessing

The wedding had been a beautiful event. Everyone had worn their finest clothes and the bride was breathtaking in her wedding garb. Family and friends had gathered together for a time of celebration and feasting. But before the guests began to eat, an elderly man made his way to the front of the celebration and stood before the bride and groom. It was the bride's grandfather. Everyone bowed their heads with respect as he placed his hands upon the bride's and groom's heads. Then he began to pray: "In the name of the Father, God of Abraham, Isaac, and Jacob; and in the name of the Son Jesus Christ…." The patriarch of the family began to bless them and their marriage.

The tradition of imparting a blessing through the laying on of hands can be traced back into ancient history. The tradition of the father blessing his son is common in many cultures to this day. It is an important rite in a young man's passage into adulthood. This is the first lesson of the fourth foundation doctrine: Laying on of Hands. It will discuss the laying on of hands to impart a blessing.

We read about a father imparting a blessing to his sons in the book of Genesis. There were two brothers who desperately wanted their father's blessing. The extremes that they went to reveal how important they felt this blessing would be.

Now Rebekah had given her husband, Isaac, twin sons. Although the two boys were twins, they were nothing alike. The elder brother had been born just minutes before the younger. Esau was everything a father would expect in an elder son. The boy grew into a strong man who loved to hunt and do things that typically would make a father proud. His younger brother, Jacob, was not big and strong nor interested in hunting. Rather, Jacob enjoyed spending time

with his mother, cooking and doing things around the camp.
As you might imagine, Isaac grew to love Esau and Rebecca
loved the younger son, Jacob. This caused a lot of tension
between the two boys.

Now it came about, that Isaac grew old and his eyes
became too dim to see. One day he called his older son Esau
and said to him, "My son. Behold now, I am old and I do
not know the day of my death. Now then, please take your
quiver and your bow, and go out to the field and hunt some
wild game for me. Prepare the meat for me in the way I
love. Then bring it to me that I may eat, so I may give you
my blessing before I die."

Rebekah was listening as Isaac spoke to his son
Esau. When Esau went to the field to hunt for game to
bring home, Rebekah said to her son Jacob, "Behold, I heard
your father speak to your brother Esau. He is going to give
your brother a blessing before he dies. Now my son, go out
to the flock and bring me two choice young goats. I will
cook them and prepare a meal that your father will love.
Then you shall bring it to your father that he may eat, so that
he may bless you before his death."

But Jacob was afraid and said, "Esau my brother is
a hairy man and I have a smooth skin. Perhaps my father
will touch my arm and discover my deceit. He will then
curse me."

But his mother said to him, "Your curse be on me,
my son. Just obey my voice; go and get them for me." So
he went and got them, and brought them to his mother. She
made some tasty food, just the way his father liked it. Then
Rebekah took the best garments of Esau her elder son,
which she had in the house, and put them on Jacob her
younger son. And she put the skins of the young goats on
his hands and on the smooth part of his neck.

So, Jacob, wearing his brother's clothes, with goat skin on his hands and neck, took the food to his blind father saying, "My father."

And Isaac said, "Here I am. Who are you, my son?"

Jacob said to his father, "I am Esau your firstborn; I have done as you told me. Get up, please. Sit and eat of my game, that you may bless me."

Isaac said to his son, "How is it that you have it so quickly, my son?"

And Jacob replied, "The Lord your God gave me success."

Then Isaac said to Jacob, "Please come close, that I may touch you, my son, to know whether you really are my son Esau or not." So, Jacob came close to Isaac his father who reached out and felt him then said, "The voice is the voice of Jacob, but the hands are the hands of Esau." Again, Isaac said, "Are you really my son Esau?"

And Jacob said, "I am."

So, he said, "Bring it to me, and I will eat of my son's game, that I may bless you." So, Isaac ate the food and drank the wine that Jacob had brought him. Then Isaac said to him, "Please come close and kiss me, my son." So, Jacob came close and kissed him; and when Isaac recognized the smell of Esau's garments, he blessed Jacob and said,

> See, the smell of my son
> Is like the smell of a field which the LORD has blessed;
> Now may God give you of the dew of heaven,

And of the fatness of the earth,
And an abundance of grain and new wine.
May peoples serve you,
And nations bow down to you.
Be master of your brothers,
And may your mother's sons bow down to you.
Cursed be those who curse you,
And blessed be those who bless you.

Now it came about, as soon as Isaac had finished blessing Jacob, he went out from the presence of Isaac his father. Just then, Esau came in from his hunting. After preparing the food he went in to his father saying, "Father, arise and eat of your son's game, that you may bless me."

Isaac said to him, "Who are you?"

And he answered, "I am your son, your firstborn, Esau."

Then Isaac trembled violently, and said, "Who was he then that hunted game and brought it to me, so that I ate of all of it before you came, and blessed him? Yes, and he shall be blessed."

When Esau heard the words of his father, he cried out with an exceedingly great and bitter cry, and said to his father, "Bless me, *even* me also, O my father!"

Then Isaac said, "Your brother came deceitfully and has taken away your blessing."

Then Esau pleaded, "Do you have only one blessing, my father? Please bless me also, my father." So, Esau lifted his voice and wept.

Then Isaac his father answered and said to him:

Behold, away from the fertility of the earth shall
be your dwelling,
And away from the dew of heaven from above.
By your sword you shall live,
And your brother you shall serve.
But it shall come about when you become
restless,
That you will break his yoke from your neck.

So, Esau bore a grudge against Jacob because of the blessing with which his father had blessed him (Gen 27:1-41).

With our mouths, we can either bless or curse. When we are filled with the Holy Spirit our words have meaning and carry with them power. The apostle Paul tells us to "bless those who persecute you; bless and do not curse…. Do not repay anyone evil for evil . . . Overcome evil with good" (Rom 12:14, 17, 21).

We should always follow the leading of the Holy Spirit. We should never be quick to lay hands on anyone and give them a blessing. Rather we should be led by God's Spirit. When he leads us to lay hands upon a person and speak a blessing into their lives, we are speaking the words of God. God's words will accomplish what he desires and achieve the purpose for which they were spoken (Isa 55:11).

This story is **important** because it shows how God views speaking blessing into another person's life, by the laying on of hands.

The **main truth** of this lesson is that at times the Holy Spirit may lead you to lay hands on a person to impart a blessing upon them. God will give you the words to say and will also fulfill the purpose for which they were spoken.

Let's **review** a few points from this lesson:

1. How can we impart a blessing to another?

A. If you said that we can lay hands on them and speak a blessing over them, then you are correct.

2. Whom did Isaac bless?

A. If you said that Isaac pronounced a blessing on Jacob and Esau, you are correct.

3. Why should we be careful in laying hands on people and pronouncing blessings?

A. If you said that words are powerful and that we should be led by the Spirit, then you are correct.

Your **assignment** for this lesson is to listen to this lesson as many times as is necessary to learn the story. Then, pray and ask God to lead you by His Holy Spirit to find someone to lay hands upon and to speak a blessing into their life.

18 Laying on of Hands: Imparting Authority

The city was a very violent place. Criminals armed with weapons would rob, injure, and even kill the citizens of the city. But on this day the mayor of the city would do something to reduce the violent crime. Gathered before him were 50 young men in uniform. They had been training for six months to become police officers. They had been taught police procedures and how to deal with crime. Each one had been issued a firearm. These 50 policemen were about to wield great power in their city. They were only missing one thing, the authority to use that power. One by one the new policemen stood before the mayor. He reached out and shook their hands and congratulated them on the completion of their training. Then he issued a police badge to each one of them. This badge would be worn on their uniforms, so that everyone would know that they had the authority to act as policemen.

This concept of a leader imparting his authority to another person can be found throughout history and in cultures around the world. In the Bible, we find many examples of authority being granted or transferred.

Now Moses was the greatest prophet in the history of Israel. He was the one God chose to deliver all of the Jewish people, who were being held in Egypt as slaves. God performed many great miracles through Moses as he led over a million descendants of Abraham out of Egypt. They set out on a journey to the land that God had promised to Abraham.

It would be on Mount Sinai that God would give to the Jewish people the Ten Commandments and the rest of the law. But the Israelites were a rebellious people. In spite of the great miracles that they had witnessed, they were afraid to enter into the land that had been promised to them.

Because of this, God pronounced a judgement upon them. Not a single adult of that generation would be allowed to enter into God's Promised Land except for Joshua and Caleb. These two men were the only ones in all of Israel who believed God and were not afraid.

So, it was that for 40 years Moses led the Israelites in the wilderness. God provided food for them and led them to water. But they never settled in any one place. Instead they lived as nomads sleeping in tents. One by one the adults who had rejected entering into God's Promised Land died. It would be their children and grandchildren who would conquer the Promised Land. Moses was now 120 years old. Only Joshua and Caleb were left from the original generation that had been delivered from Egypt.

Then the Lord said to Moses, "Go up this mountain in the Abarim Range and see the land I have given the Israelites. After you have seen it, you too will be gathered to your people and die" (Deut. 32:49-50).

Moses replied to the Lord, "May the Lord, the God who gives breath to all living things, appoint someone over this community to go out and come in before them, one who will lead them out and bring them in, so the LORD's people will not be like sheep without a shepherd."
So, the LORD said to Moses, "Take Joshua son of Nun, a man in whom is the spirit of leadership, and lay your hand on him. Have him stand before Eleazar the priest and the entire assembly and commission him in their presence. Give him some of your authority so the whole Israelite community will obey him. … At his command, he and the entire community of the Israelites will go out, and at his command they will come in."

Moses did as the LORD commanded him. He took Joshua and had him stand before Eleazar the priest and the whole assembly. Then he laid his hands on him and commissioned him, as the LORD instructed through Moses (Num 27:17-23).

This is a wonderful example of how God uses the laying on of hands as the method by which authority is transferred from one person to the next. It is important to recognize two Godly principles from this story. First, a person can only give authority that they have first received themselves. A person cannot lay hands on another and pronounce the granting of authority which they themselves do not have. The second principle that is extremely important is that God is the one who commanded Moses to lay hands on Joshua to impart authority to him. The authority never belonged to Moses. It was always God's authority and thus Moses did not have the right to give it to just anyone he chose.

It is these very principles that direct us today in the transferring of authority through the laying on of hands. Remember, Jesus said, "All authority has been given to me. Therefore, go and make disciples" (Matt 28:18-19). Any authority that we possess comes from Jesus Christ. And it must be through the guidance of the Holy Spirit that we exercise this authority or impart it to someone he chooses.

This lesson is **important** because it explains God's plan to pass his authority from one generation to the next or one people group to another.

The **main truth** of this story is that Jesus Christ has all authority, which he imparts to believers to go and make disciples. As we obey him, the Holy Spirit will lead us to impart that authority to others.

Let us **review** what this lesson has taught:
1. How can we impart authority to another?

A. If you said that we can lay hands on them and grant authority to them, then you are correct.

2. To whom did Moses transfer his authority?
A. If you said that Moses laid hands on Joshua, you answered correctly.

3. From whom does all authority flow?
A. If you said that Jesus Christ has been given all authority, then you are correct.

Your **assignment** for this lesson is to listen to this story as many times as is necessary to learn it. Then, discuss with your mentor the concept of spiritual authority within the body of Christ—his Church.

19 Laying on of Hands: To Impart the Holy Spirit

The students sat at their desks as the teacher opened the textbook and began to speak. "Today I have a wonderful gift to give you," she began. Her students suddenly looked up, giving her their attention.

One young girl raised her hand with a question: "What is the gift?" she asked.

A broad smile crossed the teacher's face as she said, "It is the gift of knowledge." A few of the children smiled back at her. Some of the children groaned to themselves. For them school was not fun or interesting. For them it was simply work that they preferred not to do. These students had no idea of the value of what the teacher held in her hands. The gift of knowledge never grows old and remains with a person their entire life.

Wouldn't it be wonderful to have a tremendous gift that you could give to people? The gift of the baptism in the Holy Spirit is second only to the gift of salvation. It is a free gift that Christ has promised to every believer who will receive it. In the New Testament Book of Acts, we read about a man who desired a gift that he could give, for *his own* benefit.

Now the city of Samaria was the ancient capital of the northern kingdom of Israel, which would become known as the region of Samaria. Jerusalem was the capital of the southern kingdom of Judah or Judea. The descendants of King David ruled Judah from Jerusalem. A variety of kings, most very wicked, had ruled the northern kingdom of Israel. This had led to deep cultural hatred between the two regions.

Soon after the Holy Spirit had been poured out on the 120 disciples in Jerusalem, a great persecution came upon the church. A Jewish religious leader, a Pharisee named Saul of Tarsus, went about arresting believers and throwing them into prison. Many of the believers in Jerusalem fled throughout Judea and Samaria, taking the gospel with them. One such godly man was Philip. He went down to a city in Samaria and proclaimed Jesus Christ there. When the crowds heard Philip, and saw the signs he performed, they all paid close attention to what he said. For with shrieks, demon spirits came out of people. Many who were paralyzed or lame were healed, so there was great joy in that city.

Now for some time a man named Simon had practiced sorcery in the city and amazed all the people of Samaria. He boasted that he was someone great. All the people, both high and low, gave him their attention and exclaimed, "This man is rightly called the Great Power of God." They followed him because he had amazed them for a long time with his sorcery. But they believed Philip as he proclaimed the good news of the kingdom of God and the name of Jesus Christ. So, they were baptized in water, both men and women. Simon himself believed and was baptized. And he followed Philip everywhere, astonished by the great signs and miracles he saw.

When the apostles in Jerusalem heard that Samaria had accepted the word of God, they sent Peter and John to Samaria. When they arrived, they prayed for the new believers there, that they might receive the Holy Spirit, because the Holy Spirit had not yet come on any of them. They had simply been baptized in water in the name of the Lord Jesus. Then Peter and John placed their hands on them, and they received the Holy Spirit.

When Simon saw that the Spirit was given at the laying on of the Apostles' hands, he offered them money and said, "Give me also this ability so that everyone on whom I lay my hands may receive the Holy Spirit."

Peter answered: "May your money perish with you, because you thought you could buy the gift of God with money! You have no part or share in this ministry, because your heart is not right before God. Repent of this wickedness and pray to the Lord in the hope that he may forgive you for having such a thought in your heart. For I see that you are full of bitterness and captive to sin."

Then Simon answered, "Pray to the Lord for me so that nothing you have said may happen to me." After they had further proclaimed the word of the Lord and testified about Jesus, Peter and John returned to Jerusalem, preaching the gospel in many Samaritan villages (Acts 8:1-25).

This is an amazing story that teaches us two very important truths. First, we learn that people can receive the baptism in the Holy Spirit through the laying on of hands. We also learn that gifts from God cannot be purchased, but are freely given and must be freely received. Every Spirit-filled believer can offer to pray and lay hands on a fellow believer to receive the baptism in the Holy Spirit. We must remember that it is not we who give the baptism, but rather Christ, the Baptizer. Remember the school teacher who offered to give the gift of knowledge to her students? Her students had to be willing to receive her teaching. In the same way, those who desire to receive the gift of the baptism in the Holy Spirit must be willing to open their hearts to receive in faith.

This story is **important** because you have learned that God uses Spirit-filled believers to lay hands on other believers and pray for them to be baptized in the Holy Spirit.

The **main truth** of this lesson is that God's gifts cannot be bought. They must be received in faith, as God freely gives them to those who ask. Christ is the Baptizer, but he often uses us to lay hands on other believers so that they may be baptized in the Holy Spirit.

Shall we **review** what this lesson has taught?
1. How can we impart the gift of the baptism in the Holy Spirit to another person?
    A. If you said that we can lay hands on them that they might receive the baptism in the Holy Spirit, then you are correct.

2. What happened to the people in Samaria when Peter and John laid hands on them?
    A. If you said that the people received the baptism in the Holy Spirit, you are correct.

3. Is it possible to purchase gifts from God?
    A. If you said, "No, gifts from God are freely given and must be freely received," then you answered correctly.

Your **assignment** for this lesson is to listen to it as many times as is necessary to learn the story. Then, if you have not yet received the baptism in the Holy Spirit, seek out your pastor or mentor and have them lay hands on you to receive this wonderful gift.

20 Laying on of Hands: To Impart Healing

A certain man bought a new car. He was so excited about his purchase. He drove it from his village to the city, carrying produce that he grew to sell in the market. One day, on the way to the market, he noticed that his car's engine was not running well. It began to sputter and smoke. The man took the car to his friend, whom he thought might be able to fix its problem. The friend looked under the bonnet and tried making adjustments. But the car continued to run poorly. Each week when the man drove to market, he would have to find a repair shop to work on his car. No one ever seemed to be able to find the problem and restore it to its original condition.

Finally, the car was running so poorly, that it was obvious that it would not make the long trip back to the village. The man was so frustrated that he decided to take the car to the original maker's repair shop. There the mechanic looked under the hood and found the problem immediately. He reconnected a rubber hose that had come loose. Suddenly the car was running as well as the day the man had purchased it.

Sickness and disease have been part of the human condition since Adam and Eve were forced from the Garden of Eden. Man has sought remedies for his illnesses through witchcraft, herbs, folk wisdom, and doctors. It seems that people will try everything but the most obvious answer. Why not ask the original Creator for help? In today's story, you will learn about how people can be healed through prayer and the laying on of hands.

The apostle Paul had been arrested and thrown into prison for preaching the gospel of Jesus Christ. Paul remained in prison for two years, while Felix was governor of Judea. But Felix was replaced by a man named Festus.

The Jewish leaders, who had first arrested Paul, saw this as an opportunity to have him executed. They appealed to Festus for a trial. This would create a significant problem for Festus. Paul was not just an inhabitant of the land; he was an actual citizen of Rome. He had specific rights. It became obvious to Paul that he would not receive a fair trial in Judea. He then exercised his rights as a Roman citizen to have his case heard before a court in Rome.

Thus, Governor Festus loaded Paul and his traveling companion, Luke, onto a boat to send him to Rome for his trial. The trip to Rome would not be without incident. Soon a terrible storm came upon their ship. The small ship was battered by the towering waves and ferocious winds for many days. The storm so darkened the sky that they could not tell night from day. On the fourteenth night, the sailors sensed that they were approaching land. Early the next morning they cut the ship's anchor and attempted to sail ashore. But the ship ran aground on a sandbar and everyone had to swim to shore. They gathered around a fire on the beach to warm their wet bodies. Paul picked up a branch to throw it into the fire. But there was a snake coiled there. It struck and latched onto Paul's arm. Paul shook the snake off into the fire. Everyone watched in horror, expecting Paul to drop dead from the snake's venom. But to their amazement, Paul did not die or get ill.

They discovered that they had landed on the island of Malta. There was an estate nearby that belonged to Publius, the chief official of the island. He welcomed them to his home and showed them generous hospitality for three days. His father was sick in bed, suffering from fever and dysentery. Paul went in to see him and, after prayer, placed his hands on him and healed him. After this had happened, the rest of the sick on the island came and were also cured. This is such a beautiful and simple account of someone being healed through prayer and the laying on of hands.

In his Gospel, Mark wrote down Jesus' final words to his disciples. He said to them, "Go into all the world and preach the gospel to all creation. Whoever believes and is baptized will be saved, but whoever does not believe will be condemned. And these signs will accompany those who believe: In my name they will drive out demons; they will speak in new tongues; they will pick up snakes with their hands; and when they drink deadly poison, it will not hurt them at all; they will lay hands on sick people, and they will get well" (Mark 16:15-18). It has been promised to us by Jesus Christ himself that we can pray and lay hands on the sick, and they will recover.

This lesson is **important** because it illustrates that since God created our bodies, we can go to him expecting a miracle of healing. Further, Jesus promised that as we lay hands on sick people, they will get well.

The **main truth** of this lesson is that believers have the authority given by Jesus to pray and lay hands on the sick, so they may be healed.

The following questions will help you **review** the lesson:

1. How can we impart healing to the sick?
      A. If you said that we can pray and lay hands on them so that they will recover, then you answered correctly.

2. Who promised the disciples that they could lay hands on the sick, who would then recover?
      A. If you said that Jesus made this promise to his disciples, you are correct.

3. What did Paul do for the suffering father of Publius?

A. If you said, "He prayed and then laid hands on him, so he was healed," then you are right.

Your **assignment** for this lesson is to listen to it and watch it as many times as is necessary to learn the story. Then, you are to find someone who is sick and after praying, lay hands on them so that they can recover from their illness.

21 Laying on of Hands: For Ordination

The football coach and his assistant stood in front of the group of young men. The boys had all been demonstrating their skills for the coaches, hoping that they would be chosen for the local football team. Adroa was one of the young men who waited nervously. A large box sat at the assistant coach's feet. Adroa knew there were team uniforms in the box. He had played football since he was very young, but had never been on a real team or worn a football uniform. Adroa was desperate to be chosen. He just knew that if he were given a uniform, it would make him a real football player. The coach looked down at his papers and then called a name. The young man next to Adroa stepped forward and shook the coach's hand. The assistant coach reached into the box, pulled out a uniform, and handed it the young man. Name after name was called until the uniform box was empty. Adroa was brokenhearted. His name had not been called. He would not become a real football player that day.

Often people think that if they were just given a title, they could be successful. It is not the title that brings success, but rather the skills and abilities of the person. In the kingdom of God, we also find this to be true. Many young people seek credentials and ordination. They mistakenly believe that once they have received the endorsement of the church, they will be successful in ministry.

On the Day of Pentecost, the Holy Spirit came upon the disciples in Jerusalem and the Church was born. The Early Church enjoyed tremendous growth in Jerusalem, until the Jewish religious leaders rose up against them with great persecution. Many believers were arrested and imprisoned. Believers fled Jerusalem, leaving behind only the Apostles. Some of the believers eventually traveled to

the city of Antioch, located in the modern country of
Turkey. Soon a growing church was thriving in Antioch.
Believers were first called Christians in Antioch.

In the church at Antioch were prophets and teachers.
Among them were Barnabas and Saul of Tarsus—who
would become known as the apostle Paul. Now Barnabas
and Paul were well known within the church. They were
respected teachers of Christ with proven ministries.

While the leaders were ministering to the Lord and
fasting, a prophetic word was given through the Holy Spirit:
"Set apart for me Barnabas and Saul for the work to which I
have called them." The leaders then fasted and prayed to
confirm the prophetic word. Finding agreement in their
hearts, they called Paul and Barnabas before them. They laid
hands on them and ordained them to the work God had
called them to.

Paul and Barnabas then set out on their first
missionary journey. They preached the Good News of
Christ in many cities and they established churches (Acts
13:2-3).

This very brief story is found in the New Testament
Book of Acts. It gives us insight into God's process of
ordination. Let's follow Paul's story to see what we can
learn. First, we know that God had previously called Paul
to ministry and that he had then gone through a time of
preparation. He had been mentored by Barnabas and
became involved in ministry within the local church at
Antioch. The church recognized his ministry as being from
God. He and Barnabas took aid to the starving Christians in
Jerusalem. Yet Paul still did not try to advance his own
ministry, but waited upon God with Bible study, prayer, and
fasting. It was God, the Holy Spirit, who revealed to the

leadership that it was time for Paul and Barnabas to move out into their own ministry.

We think about the godly leaders of Antioch, worshiping the Lord. When God spoke clearly that it was time for Paul and Barnabas to be set apart, the prophets and teachers did not rashly lay hands upon them. Instead, they prayed and fasted more. Then they called Paul and Barnabas before them. Placing their hands on them, the leaders ordained them to the work God had called them to and sent them off.

From this we see that the laying on of hands for ordination does not prepare a person for ministry. It is rather a public recognition of the work that God has called and already equipped a person to do. Different parts of the body of Christ have various traditions in the setting apart of ministers. As you prepare yourself for the ministry to which God has called you and submit to church leaders, he will confirm your readiness to receive their blessing. God has a plan and he also has a time for that plan to unfold in your life.

This story is **important** because it clearly explains how God calls people into his work and how the church acknowledges and blesses the minister who is prepared already for the task. It is God who calls laborers and the Church that sets them apart for ministry.

The **main truth** of this lesson is that the Holy Spirit will choose and direct people for ministry as believers' worship, fast, and pray for God to lead them. In his time, he will open the doors for ministry.

Let's **review** this story from the Book of Acts,

1. In what city were Paul and Barnabas ministering, before they began their missionary work?

A. If you said that Paul and Barnabas were ministering in the city of Antioch, then you answered correctly.

2. Who ordained Paul and Barnabas to do their missionary work?

A. If you said that the leaders of the church in Antioch ordained them, you are right.

3. How did the church leaders of Antioch ordain Paul and Barnabas to the work God had called them to?

A. If you said, "They prayed and fasted, then laid hands on them," you are correct.

Your **assignment** for this lesson is to listen to this lesson as many times as is necessary to learn the story. Then, examine your own life, ministry, and calling. Ponder these questions. Where are you in God's process? Do you have a clear call from God? Have you been working hard to prepare for ministry? Are you actively involved in ministry in your local church? Are you fasting and praying for further direction from the Holy Spirit through your leaders?

22 Resurrection of the Dead - Jesus

A Christian song that was popular a few years ago talks about one thing that makes Christianity different from other major religions. It says that you can visit the tombs of the founders of other religions and find their bones there. But if you visit the tomb of Jesus, you will find that it is empty. He is risen! He is risen indeed! Thus far we have learned the first four foundation doctrines of the church. Those are: Repentance, Faith, Baptisms, and Laying on of Hands. Today we will begin discussing the fifth foundation doctrine: The Resurrection of the Dead.

God commanded the Israelites to have seven celebrations or feasts each year. The first was the Feast of Passover. It happens every spring on the fourteenth day of the first month of the Jewish calendar. It is a feast of salvation and was given to the Jews as a reminder of God delivering the Israelites out of Egyptian bondage.

The second feast was to begin the very next day and it was to run for seven days. It was called the Feast of Unleavened Bread. Leaven, or yeast, is what causes bread dough to rise. When the Jews fled Egypt, they did not have time to allow their bread dough to rise. They were forced to cook their bread without yeast.

The third feast of the year happened on the first day of the week following the first Sabbath of the Feast of Unleavened Bread. This feast is called the Feast of First Fruits. Spring had come to the land and certain plants were already bearing fruit or grain. The Israelites were commanded to take some of this early barley and flax harvest and bring it unto the Lord as a sacrifice. This early harvest was not the main harvest. That would come seven weeks later during the fifth feast—the Feast of Pentecost, also called Feast of Weeks.

Then the largest harvest of the year would happen at the end of summer during the Feast of Trumpets. Each of these feasts plays a significant role in God's supernatural calendar of eternal events. Students of the Bible have understood that at the time of Christ, the Jews had several different calendar systems in use. One was the agricultural or civil calendar. Then there were several religious Hebrew calendars, depending on whether the person was more conservative or more liberal. This helps to understand the various names used for the months and various interpretations given to the feast days by the writers of the Gospels.

Matthew, Mark, and Luke agree that Jesus' last supper with his 12 disciples was their celebration of the Passover Feast and took place on Thursday evening. Later that night Jesus was betrayed and arrested in the Garden of Gethsemane. The Feast of Unleavened Bread would have begun the following day, Friday. It was this Friday when Jesus was dragged before the Roman Governor, Pontius Pilate, and was sentenced to death. Since the next day would be the Jewish high sabbath it was very important to the Jews that Jesus be crucified on that Friday and that he should be dead and buried before night fell. And so, it was. Jesus was crucified early Friday morning around nine. He hung upon the cross and died at three in the afternoon. One of the Jewish leaders, a righteous man, asked the Roman governor for Jesus' body, to bury it. Governor Pilate was surprised that Jesus was already dead, but after confirming Jesus' death, released his body for burial.

It was the Jewish tradition to bury their dead on the same day the person died. The body would be wrapped in clean cloth with spices to reduce the odor of decay. Caves, or tombs carved into the rock, would be used as a temporary resting place for the dead. There the body would decay until only the bones were left. It was then that the family would open the tomb and carefully collect the bones. After wrapping them with new cloth, they respectfully placed the bones into a small stone box and replaced them in the tomb. By this method a family tomb would be used many times. But it was late in the afternoon when Jesus' body was released for burial. There was no time to properly prepare his body with spices. Instead he was quickly wrapped with clean cloths and then placed into a brand-new tomb that had never been used before.

The sun set that Friday evening and all of the Apostles and believers were in shock and deep despair. It was the supposed to be the beginning of the Feast of Unleavened Bread—a time of happiness and joy. Instead it was time of incredible sorrow. The next day was Saturday, the Jewish Sabbath or 'Holy Day.' The following day would be the first day of the week after the Sabbath of the Feast of Unleavened Bread. This was the beginning day of God's third feast, the Feast of First Fruits. While the Jews prepared to bring their First Fruits harvest offering to the Temple, God was preparing his own First Fruits. For it was early Sunday morning that the unbelievable happened. Jesus Christ's body had been supernaturally transformed. He had been resurrected from the dead! The disciple Matthew wrote that tombs were opened and the bodies of many saints who had died were also raised to life, like Lazarus had been raised. And coming out of the tombs after his resurrection, they entered the holy city.

Christ's resurrection is God's First Fruits resurrection. Jesus conquered death through his redemptive work on the Cross. Paul preached that Christ had to suffer and was "the first to rise from the dead" (Acts 26:23). He taught the Corinthians, saying, "Christ has indeed been raised from the dead, the First Fruits of those who have fallen asleep. For since death came through a man, the resurrection of the dead comes also through a man. For as in Adam all die, so in Christ all will be made alive. But each in turn: Christ, the First Fruits; then, when he comes, those who belong to him" (1Cor 15:20-23). Jesus' resurrection is the demonstration of the promise made to every believer, that we too will one day be resurrected from the dead. And we will be with our resurrected Lord for all eternity.

This story is **important** because it gives us insight into God's plan for his Son Jesus, and God's promise to those who believe in him. Because Christ lives, we also shall live!

The **main truth** of this lesson is that God has planned the events of his timetable so that significant New Testament events took place on special days of the Old Testament calendar. He intended for us to see Christ's resurrection as the First Fruits of those who have died and will be raised in supernatural spirit bodies.

To **review** this lesson, answer the following questions:

1. What was the third feast in the Jewish calendar?
      A. If you answered, "The Feast of First Fruits," you answered correctly.

2. What was God's First Fruits harvest at the time of Jesus' death?
      A. If you said that Jesus' resurrection from the dead is considered to be God's First Fruits, you are correct.

3. What is the fifth Foundation Doctrine?
      A. If you said, "Resurrection of the Dead is the fifth Foundation Doctrine," then you are right.

Your **assignment** for this lesson is to listen to this lesson as many times as is necessary to learn the story. You should be able to clearly explain the concept of Jesus' resurrection from the dead as being a First Fruits promise of God that we will also one day be resurrected from the dead. Memorize First Corinthians 15:20-23: "Christ has indeed been raised from the dead, the First Fruits of those who have fallen asleep. For since death came through a man, the resurrection of the dead comes also through a man. For as in Adam all die, so in Christ all will be made alive. But each in turn: Christ, the First Fruits; then, when he comes, those who belong to him" Find a few people and teach them this important principle.

23 Resurrection of the Dead – The Rapture

In our last lesson, you learned that God commanded the Jewish people to have seven feasts or celebrations each year. The first month of the traditional Jewish calendar happens in spring. Thus, the first feast, Passover, happened in the first month of the Jewish calendar. We remember that Jesus was crucified at Passover, buried during the Feast of Unleavened Bread, and was resurrected on the Sunday of the Feast of First Fruits. Jesus' resurrection was the promise and proof to all believers that the resurrection of the dead would one day occur and that all believers would be raised from the dead.

The fourth feast of the Jewish calendar is called "Pentecost." It happens 49 days after First Fruits Sunday. On First Fruits, the Jews would present an offering of barley unto God from the early harvest. The first complete harvest, the wheat harvest, happened seven weeks later. So the Feast of Pentecost was when the Jews gathered in Jerusalem to present an offering unto God in thanks for the completion of that wheat harvest. It was on the Feast of Pentecost that God poured out upon the Church his gift of the Baptism in the Holy Spirit.

After Pentecost, the Jews would return to their villages and prepare for the harvest of grapes, pomegranates, figs, and olives. The Jews were commanded to return to Jerusalem for the Feast of Trumpets. Sometime at the end of September or early October, the Jewish high priest would blow a trumpet announcing that all of Israel should cease harvesting and come to Jerusalem to present their offerings unto the Lord. Some Christians believe that the next great event in God's eternal calendar will happen some year during this feast. This great event is called the Rapture of the Church. Just as Jesus was resurrected on the Jewish feast of First Fruits, it is believed that someday during the Feast of Trumpets, God will harvest the earth and resurrect the dead believers just as Christ was resurrected. Jesus clearly taught his disciples, however, that no one knows the day nor the hour of the Rapture, not even the angels in heaven, only the Father (Mark 13:32).

Now the apostle Paul planted a church in the city of Corinth which is west of Athens, Greece. From there he traveled about 275 kilometers (125 miles) east to modern day Turkey and planted a church in the city of Ephesus. Paul would remain in Ephesus for three years while he taught and built up the local believers. While in Ephesus he received news of problems that the young believers in Corinth were experiencing. So, Paul wrote a very long detailed letter to them. He gave them fatherly instruction and correction in their faith and their behavior. Among the issues he addressed was the subject of the resurrection of the dead.

It would seem that someone in Corinth was teaching people that there would not be a resurrection of the dead. This was obviously incorrect, but whoever was teaching this must have been very persuasive. Here are some of the things Paul wrote to the Corinthians:

"For, what I received I passed on to you as of first importance: that Christ died for our sins according to the Scriptures, that he was buried, that he was raised on the third day according to the Scriptures, and that he appeared to Peter, then to the Twelve. After that, he appeared to more than five hundred of the brothers and sisters at one time, most of whom are still living, though some have fallen asleep. Then he appeared to James, then to all the apostles, and last of all, he appeared to me also, as to one untimely born. …

"But if it is preached that Christ has been raised
from the dead, how can some of you say that there is no
resurrection of the dead? If there is no resurrection of the
dead, then not even Christ has been raised. And if Christ has
not been raised, our preaching is useless and so is your faith.
…

"But Christ has indeed been raised from the dead,
the First Fruits of those who have fallen asleep. For
since death came through a man, the resurrection of the dead
comes also through a man. For as in Adam all die, so
in Christ all will be made alive. But each in turn: Christ, the
First Fruits; then, when he comes, those who belong to him.
…

"So, will it be with the resurrection of the dead. The
body that is sown is perishable, it is raised imperishable; it is
sown in dishonor, it is raised in glory; it is sown in
weakness, it is raised in power; it is sown a natural body, it
is raised a spiritual body. …

"I declare to you, brothers and sisters, that flesh and
blood cannot inherit the kingdom of God, nor does the
perishable inherit the imperishable. Listen, I tell you
a mystery: We will not all sleep, but we will all
be changed—in a flash, in the twinkling of an eye, at the last
trumpet. For the trumpet will sound, the dead will be
raised imperishable, and we will be changed. For
the perishable must clothe itself with the imperishable, and
the mortal with immortality" (1Cor 15: 3-4, 12-14, 20-23,
42-44, 50-53).

The apostle Paul clearly teaches that one day Christ
will return for his Church. The most amazing thing will
happen! Everyone who has died a believer will suddenly
come back to life. It will not be their old bones or rotted
flesh, but rather, in a single moment they will come to life

with a brand-new supernatural body. It will be a spirit body like Jesus' glorified body. Paul teaches that any believer who is alive at this moment will also suddenly be transformed. They will be changed in a blink of the eye. Suddenly their human body of flesh and bone will be transformed into the supernatural body that will never become sick, will never age, but will be in the presence of God forever.

We can know a little of what this body will be like from what the Bible teaches us about what Jesus was able to do after his resurrection. Jesus was able to eat and drink. He also was able to appear and then disappear. Walls and doors were not able to keep him out of a locked room. Finally, his disciples watched as he floated up into the sky and out of sight. We can assume that all of the things that limit our human bodies will not apply to our supernatural resurrected ones.

And rightly so. We were created and intended to become God's children. God is a spirit being. We also have spirits, but right now our human bodies limit us. One day we will all receive a supernatural spirit body and thus we will be in the presence of our Father forever.

This lesson is **important** because it explains the blessed hope of all who follow Christ. Whether you die before Christ comes back for the Church or whether you are alive at that time, you will receive a supernatural spirit body. And so, shall we ever be with the Lord.

The **main truth** of this lesson is that God's timetable is settled, and believers must be ready to meet him in the air when he comes for his Church.

To **review** this lesson, please answer these questions:

1. What is the Rapture of the Church?

      A. If you said that the Rapture of the Church is when Christ returns for the Church, then you are correct.

2. What will happen to those believers who have already died, at the Rapture?

      A. If you said, "The dead in Christ will be resurrected from the dead and given a supernatural body," you are correct.

3. What happens to believers who are alive at the time of the Rapture?

      A. If you said that believers who are alive at the Rapture will be instantly transformed and receive supernatural bodies, then you are correct.

      Your **assignment** for this lesson is to listen to it at least three times until you clearly understand the Rapture of the Church and the resurrection of believers. Find a few believers and discuss this truth with them.

24 Resurrection of the Dead – The Return

In our last two lessons, we have learned that Jesus was the First Fruits of the resurrection of the dead and that all believers, both dead and living, will one day be instantaneously changed into supernatural spirit beings at the Rapture. The Bible teaches us that we will meet Christ in the air at the Rapture. Many scholars teach that after the Rapture of the Church a terrible time of tribulation will come upon the earth for seven years. The Church will be gone from the earth and God's wrath will be poured out upon those left behind. During these seven years of Tribulation some people will realize that Christ is the Lord and will believe on him. These Christians will go through a time of great persecution and many will be martyred.

God revealed to the apostle John that these seven years would begin with a horrific war. One-quarter of the world's population will die because of the war. Some will die because of wounds received in battle. Many civilians will die because of famine and diseases caused by the war. But this is just the beginning of the seven years of the Tribulation. Next may be an impact of an asteroid or comet. This massive object will hit the ocean traveling perhaps 90,000 kilometers per hour. Massive tsunamis will destroy one-third of all of the ships at sea. One-third of the sea life will perish as well. The heat from the impact will set on fire all of the grass on the earth and one-third of all of the trees. Acid rain will fall upon one-third of the earth, poisoning the rivers, lakes, and even underground streams. A black cloud will cover one-third of the earth, plunging the earth into darkness.

Because of these terrible events an army of 200 million men will go to war. Perhaps an entire civilization may be forced to relocate, because their waters have become poisonous. The end result of this massive army and the war that ensues is that one-third of the remaining population of the earth will die. Over one-half of the entire earth's population will have died since the Rapture of the Church.

But the end still will not have come. Satan himself will be cast down to the earth and will cause great political intrigue leading to a one-world government. At the end of the seven years of tribulation the Bible says that Jesus will appear in the clouds with a great army clothed in white. Some people believe that this great army are the raptured saints. Others believe that they are all of the angels of heaven. Either way, Jesus will return in great power and glory. This is referred to as the Second Coming of Christ. The apostle John wrote this about it:

> I saw heaven standing open and there before me was a white horse, whose rider is called Faithful and True. With justice he judges and wages war. His eyes are like blazing fire, and on his head are many crowns. He has a name written on him that no one knows but he himself. He is dressed in a robe dipped in blood, and his name is the Word of God. The armies of heaven were following him, riding on white horses and dressed in fine linen, white and clean. Coming out of his mouth is a sharp sword with which to strike down the nations. He will rule them with an iron scepter. He treads the winepress of the fury of the wrath of God Almighty. On his robe and on his thigh, he has this name written: "KING OF KINGS, AND LORD OF LORDS" (Rev 19:11-16).

The apostle Matthew recorded Jesus saying this about his return:

> Immediately after the tribulation of those days 'the sun will be darkened, and the moon will

not give its light; the stars will fall from heaven, and the powers of the heavens will be shaken.'

Then the sign of the Son of Man will appear in heaven, and then all the tribes of the earth will mourn, and they will see the Son of Man coming on the clouds of heaven with power and great glory. And He will send His angels with a great sound of a trumpet, and they will gather together His elect from the four winds, from one end of heaven to the other (Matt 24:29-31, NKJV).

What we know is this, when Jesus returns to this earth, he will gather to himself all of the remaining believers upon the earth, both the living, and those who died during the tribulation. They will all participate in the resurrection of the believers. They will all receive supernatural spirit bodies and they will be part of Christ's kingdom forever. And with this, the first resurrection is complete. It began with Christ who was the First fruits of God's resurrection. Then came the Rapture of the church. And finally, the resurrection of all believers was complete at Christ's return to the earth.

This lesson is **important** because it explains the difference between the Rapture of the Church and the Second Coming of Christ for those martyred and those believers still living at the end of the Tribulation. When Jesus comes with the Saints and the last group of believers is transformed, this completes the first resurrection.

The **main truth** of this lesson is that Christians should be ready to meet the Lord in the air at the Rapture. Though the suffering will be great, some will still be saved during the Tribulation and resurrected at the Second Coming.

Let's **review** what you have learned in this lesson:

1. Who was the First Fruits of God's resurrection power?

A. If you said that Jesus was the First Fruits of God's resurrection, then you are correct.

2. Who are resurrected and changed at the Rapture?

A. If you said that the dead in Christ will be resurrected first, then we who are still alive will be transformed, and caught up to meet the Lord in the air, you are correct.

3. How is the first resurrection completed?

A. If you said that believers who came to Christ during the Tribulation are resurrected and transformed when Christ returns to the earth, then you are correct.

Your **assignment** for this lesson is to listen to this lesson at least three times until you clearly understand the progression of events that are tied to the resurrection of believers. Then continue your discussion with the few believers with whom you previously discussed the resurrection.

25 Resurrection of the Dead – The Wicked

The king had led his army off to war. He knew that he would be gone for at least a year, perhaps two. Before he left, he called together his leaders and appointed them to rule over the land in his absence. Two years later the king returned to find his kingdom in chaos. He then sat upon his throne and began to call the people of his kingdom to come to his court. Over a few months' time he had called everyone. He spoke to those who had been loyal to him, and those who had caused trouble and had been rebellious. In order for the king to pass judgment, everyone had to appear before the throne. And in a similar way, one day the King will sit upon his Great White Throne and call all of mankind before him to be judged.

Now, the return of Jesus to the earth completes the three phases of the First Resurrection. The three phases are: 1) Jesus' resurrection which was the First Fruits resurrection. It also served as the proof of the promise that all of Christ's followers would one day be resurrected. 2) The second phase of this resurrection will be the Rapture of the Church. And, 3) the last part of this resurrection will be when Christ returns to the earth. All three of these make up what is called the First Resurrection. The apostle John wrote, "Blessed and holy are those who have part in the first resurrection. The second death has no power over them, but they will be priests of God and of Christ and will reign with him for a thousand years" (Rev 20:6). This is important to understand, since Jesus taught that there would be a Second Resurrection. In this lesson, we will learn about the Second Resurrection.

Jesus will return to the earth, leading a tremendous heavenly army. Satan, the fallen cherub that has deceived the entire world, will be captured, bound, and thrown into a bottomless pit, where he will be imprisoned for 1000 years.

Jesus will set up his throne in Jerusalem where with the help of the resurrected believers, he will rule over all of the earth. These 1000 years are called the Millennium. Now all the earth will be populated with the unbelievers who survived the seven years of tribulation. Jesus and the saints will rule over them for the entire Millennium. At the end of the 1000 years, Satan will be released for a short season. He will stir up all of the unbelievers and will lead a revolt against Jesus and the saints. But Christ will call down fire from heaven which will devour them all. It is at this time that the history of mankind upon the earth will come to an end and the time of judgment will begin.

This is what the apostle John saw in his vision which he recorded in the Book of Revelation:

> Then I saw a great white throne and Him who sat upon it, from whose face the earth and the heaven fled away. And there was found no place for them. And I saw the dead, small and great, standing before God, and books were opened. And another book was opened, which is the Book of Life. And the dead were judged according to their works, by the things which were written in the books. The sea gave up the dead who were in it, and Death and Hades delivered up the dead who were in them. And they were judged, each one according to his works (Rev 20:11-13, NKJV).

There will be a Second Resurrection of the dead. It will happen right before the Great White Throne Judgment. This resurrection will be the resurrection of the unbelievers—the wicked dead. They will be brought back to life to stand before God for judgment. Indeed, blessed are those who have a part in the First Resurrection. Those who have a part in the Second Resurrection will have to stand before God for eternal judgment. In our next four lessons, we will learn what the Bible teaches about eternal judgment.

This lesson is **important** because you have learned how those who die without Christ will be resurrected and will stand before God to be judged for their deeds.

The **main truth** of this lesson is that unbelievers too will receive supernatural spirit bodies at the time of the Second Resurrection. These wicked are raised to appear before the Great White Throne judgment.

To **review** the lesson, answer the following questions:
1. What are the three parts of the First Resurrection?
      A. If you said that Jesus' resurrection, the Rapture, and the Return of Christ comprise the First Resurrection, then you are right.

2. Who will be resurrected in the Second Resurrection?
      A. If you said, "The wicked will be resurrected from the dead in the Second Resurrection," you are correct.

3. Why are the wicked resurrected from the dead?
      A. If you answered that the wicked are resurrected from the dead in order for them to be judged, then you answered correctly.

26 Eternal Judgment – Christ the Judge

The man stood in the courtroom facing the judge. He was accused of breaking the law. The government's attorney had presented the case for the prosecution. The man's attorney had presented a defense. All of the testimony, presenting of evidence, and recitation of the law were finished. The man stood before the judge who would give judgment. The man was terrified. The judge looked down on the man and pronounced his judgment. The law had clearly been broken. The law clearly stated that the man must pay an enormous fine or be sentenced to prison. The man hung his head in shame. His wife and young daughter began to weep. They knew that he had no money to pay the fine and that he would be going to prison for a long time. What do you think happened to the man? We will find out later in this lesson.

In the Book of Hebrews, we find this verse. "It is appointed for men to die once, but after this the judgment" (Heb 9:27). Every human whom has ever lived has two appointments that they will not escape from. The first appointment is death. The second appointment is standing before the throne of Christ, the Judge.

The apostle John recorded Jesus saying this about himself:

> The Father judges no one, but has given all judgment to the Son, that all may honor the Son, even as they honor the Father. He who does not honor the Son does not honor the Father who sent him. Truly, truly, I say to you, he who hears my word, and believes him who sent me, has eternal life; he does not come into judgment, but has passed from death to life.

Truly, truly, I say to you, the hour is coming, and now is, when the dead will hear the voice of the Son of God, and those who hear will live. For as the Father has life in himself, so he has granted the Son also to have life in himself, and has given him authority to execute judgment, because he is the Son of man. Do not marvel at this; for the hour is coming when all who are in the tombs will hear his voice and come forth, those who have done good, to the resurrection of life, and those who have done evil, to the resurrection of judgment.

I can do nothing on my own authority; I hear, I judge; and my judgment is just, because I seek not my own will but the will of him who sent me (John 5:22-30, RSV).

Knowing that we will one day be judged by Jesus Christ, the King, is a very sobering thought. The Bible teaches us that our deeds will be judged. It would seem that by doing good deeds we can find favor with God. But we must study the teachings of Christ in their entirety to understand what judgment lies before us.

The apostle Paul wrote "For all have sinned and fall short of the glory of God" (Rom 3:23). The prophet Isaiah wrote "For all of us have become like one who is unclean, and all our righteous acts are like filthy rags" (Isa 64:6). Paul again wrote "For the wages of sin is death, but the gift of God is eternal life in Christ Jesus our Lord" (Rom 6:23).

From these verses and many more, we learn that good deeds alone cannot remove the guilt and judgment that we deserve because of our sins. God's law clearly states that the payment for sin is death. But the apostle Peter explains God's remedy for the demand of his law. "For Christ also suffered once for sins, the just for the unjust, that he might bring us to God" (1Peter 3:18). Christ gives life even now.

The spiritually dead person who hears him receives life from him. We can know that we have eternal life. On that day when we will all stand before Jesus Christ, the Judge, the first question that must be answered is whether a person accepted Jesus Christ as their Lord and Savior.

Remember the story we began this lesson with? The man standing before the judge was in dire trouble. The law demanded that he pay a fine or go to prison. It was impossible for the man to pay the fine. As his wife and daughter wept, the judge demanded that the man pay the fine or present himself for imprisonment. The man could not lift his head to face the judge. In great shame and embarrassment, he whispered, "I cannot pay the fine." The judge then did the unexpected. He reached into his own pocket and removed from his wallet a large amount of money. He offered it to the man, saying, "Here is the money to pay the price for your crime."

What do you think the man should do? Accept the free gift? What do you think the judge should do if the man rejects the gift? In the same way, Jesus Christ the Judge has already paid the price for our sins by dying on the cross in our place. He freely offers us this gift of salvation. Those who reject Christ have destined themselves to judgment.

This lesson is **important** because it clearly teaches from Scripture that every person deserves God's judgment for their sins. It just as plainly shows that Jesus already paid the price for our sins and took our judgment on the Cross.

The **main truth** of this lesson is that we can be saved by believing in Christ as our Lord, and receive the gift of eternal life.

The following questions will help you to **review** the lesson you have heard:

1. The book of Hebrews says that everyone is appointed to die and face what?

A. If you said, "Everyone is appointed to die once and after that comes judgment," then you are correct.

2. Who does the Bible teach will be the judge of all humanity?

A. If you said that Jesus Christ has been appointed the judge of all, you are correct.

3. Is doing good deeds enough to avoid eternal judgment?

A. If you answered, "No, only through Jesus Christ can we be saved," then you answered correctly.

Your **assignment** for this lesson is to listen to this lesson three times and then teach someone else about Jesus Christ, the Judge of all the earth.

27 Eternal Judgment – Judgment of the Saints

Jesus told a parable about judgment. He said that the kingdom of heaven is like this. There was a great man who was going on a long trip. He called his own servants to him, so that he could entrust to them his wealth. Each man had different skills and abilities, so the master entrusted to each of them a quantity of gold that they were capable of managing. The first man was given five bags of gold coins, the second man two bags of gold coins, and the third man was given one bag of gold coins. All three men knew what was expected of them. Then the great man left on his journey, leaving the three servants to manage his wealth.

The first two men quickly set about investing the master's money. But for some reason the third man could not decide what to do with the gold. Eventually he buried the gold in the ground to keep it safe. Sometime later the rich man returned and called his servants to give an account. The first servant said, "Master, you entrusted five bags of gold coins to me. See, I have managed your money well and have doubled it. You now have ten bags of gold coins."

The master was very pleased with his servant and said, "Well done, good and faithful servant. You were faithful in a little, so I will put you in charge of much more."

Then the second servant presented himself before the rich man. "Master, you entrusted to me two bags of gold coins. I have doubled your investment and now you have four bags of gold."

Again, the master was pleased and said, "Well done, good and faithful servant. You were faithful in a little, so I will put you in charge of much."

Finally, the third servant came before the rich man and said, "Master, you entrusted to me a bag of gold coins. I knew that you expected a profit, but I was afraid so I hid your money to keep it safe. Here is your bag of gold."

The master became very angry and said, "You lazy and wicked servant. You knew that I expected a profit, but you have done nothing! You did not even put my money in the bank, so that I at least would have received interest on it. He then told his men, "Take the bag of gold coins from this worthless servant and give it to the man with the ten bags of gold. He knows what to do with my wealth. Then, take this worthless servant and cast him out of my presence" (Matt 25:14-30).

From this story, we learn that the servants of the master will be judged according to their obedience. All three servants belonged to the master. They all understood what was expected from them. Two were obedient. One was not.

Every believer will stand before the Judgment Seat of Christ where he will judge their works and reward them for their faithfulness. This judgment is not determining their salvation, but rather is a judgment of their works. The apostle Paul wrote to the church in Corinth to teach them about how their work for Christ would one day be judged:

> Each will be rewarded according to his own labor. For we are God's fellow workers; you are God's field, God's building.
> By the grace God has given to me, I laid a foundation as an expert builder, and someone else is building on it. But each one must be careful how he builds. For no one can lay any foundation other than the one already laid, which is Jesus Christ. If any man builds on this foundation using gold,

silver, costly stones, wood, hay, or straw, his work will be shown for what it is, because the Day will bring it to light. It will be revealed with fire, and the fire will test the quality of each man's work. If what he has built survives, he will receive his reward. If it is burned up, he will suffer loss; he himself will be saved, but only as one escaping through the flames (1Cor 3:8-15).

These concepts of a believer working for an eternal reward are very important. Now someone may argue that Paul said, "For it is by grace you have been saved, through faith—and this is not from yourselves, it is the gift of God—not by works, so that no one can boast" (Eph 2:8-9). And indeed, we are saved by faith in Jesus Christ. But we must also remember that our works will be judged.

The apostle James taught that true faith would produce good works. He wrote this:

> What good is it, my brothers and sisters, if someone claims to have faith but has no deeds? Can such faith save them? Suppose a brother or a sister is without clothes and daily food. If one of you says to them, 'Go in peace, keep warm and well fed,' but does nothing about their physical needs, what good is it? In the same way, faith by itself, if it is not accompanied by action, is dead.
> But someone will say, 'You have faith; I have deeds.'
> Show me your faith without deeds, and I will show you my faith by my deeds. You believe that there is one God. Good! Even the demons believe that—and shudder.

James went on to give evidence that faith without works is useless. He concluded, "For as the body without the spirit is dead, so faith without works is dead also" (James 2:14-19, 26).

Faith is not possible without works. True faith will express itself through love. Martin Luther explained that a person is justified—declared righteous before God—by faith alone, but not by a faith that is alone. Genuine faith will produce good works, but only faith in Christ saves.

This story is **important** because it points to the truth that our obedience and faithfulness matters to God. Those who show their faith through their good works will be rewarded at the Judgment Seat of Christ.

The **main truth** of this lesson is although we are saved by grace, through faith, God expects us to do his works while we live for him on this earth.

To **review** the points of this lesson, memorize the following questions:

1. Jesus taught that every believer's works would be judged. Does this judgment determine a believer's salvation?
   A. If you said no, a believer's deeds will be judged to determine their reward, but they will be saved, then you are correct.

2. What did the Apostle James teach about faith and works?
   A. If you said that faith without works is dead, you are correct.

3. In the parable of the master entrusting gold to his servants, what was the reward that the faithful servants received?
   A. If you said that they were given greater responsibility, then you are correct.

Let me tell you about a man who was liked by everyone. He had only one real flaw; he loved to get drunk. It didn't matter whether it was beer, wine, or liquor, he would drink it all. When he was drunk, he would forget about all of his troubles. He was one of those people who became very happy when they were drunk. He would laugh, tell stories, sing songs, and even dance when he was drunk. His drinking friends called him the "life of the party." Now he only lived a few kilometers from his favorite bar. Each week when he received his paycheck, he would drive to the bar to meet his friends. They would drink and party late into the evening. Then, stumbling from the bar, he would get into his small truck and drive home.

This had been his weekly routine for many years, but it all changed one tragic night. While driving home drunk, he lost control of his truck and collided head-on with a small car. The man did not remember anything from the accident. He awoke to find himself in the local jail. He was accused of manslaughter. The driver of the car he had collided with had died. The man hated being in jail. His jail cell was small and the food was not very good. He remained in the local jail for many weeks, until he finally went to court and faced the judge. There was no defense for his actions. The judge found him guilty and sentenced him to life in prison. The man had hated the local jail, but it was nothing compared to the harsh conditions of prison. He would live out the rest of his life in agony and suffering.

The Bible says that God "will bring every deed into judgment, including every hidden thing, whether it is good or evil" (Eccl 12:14). Every living being which has ever been created, including the angels, will one day be judged. Some people think that hell is the eternal place of punishment. But this is not correct. Hell is the unpleasant place where the wicked dead await their final judgment. In some ways, it is like being in jail awaiting your day before the judge. There are also people who believe that Satan lives in hell. But this also is incorrect. No one, neither Satan, demons, nor the wicked, enjoys hell.

The Bible teaches us that Satan is our adversary. The name 'Satan,' in Hebrew, actually means 'the accuser.' In the Book of Revelation, John says that Satan is the accuser of the saints. He stands before God day and night trying to accuse believers of sins. Satan much prefers being in heaven to being in hell. Beginning in the Book of Job, we see Satan in heaven, lying and accusing a righteous man of God (Job 1:9-11). Again, in Zechariah, Satan accuses the high priest and Jehovah rebukes him (Zech. 3:1-2).

But the day will come when Satan will be judged and punished. It is prophesied that one day there will be a great Tribulation that will last for seven years. Halfway through the Tribulation, there will be a great war in heaven. Michael, the archangel, and the angels of God will war with Satan and his fallen angels. Satan will lose and he will be cast down to the earth. For three and one-half years he will rule over the entire earth through a man who is called the beast. Satan will also give power to another man, who will be called the false prophet. Together these three will rule the earth and persecute the Jewish nation for three and one-half years. In a previous lesson we learned that Christ will return to the earth at the end of the seven years of the Great Tribulation. The beast and the false prophet will be cast alive into an eternal place of punishment called the lake of fire. If hell is the local jail, then the lake of fire is the horrific prison from which no one can escape. It is a place of great suffering and torment that is beyond imagination. It was created specifically as an eternal place of punishment for Satan and his fallen angels. Who can comprehend a place where one is constantly being burned alive and yet never dies? Yet this is their destiny.

We have learned that at Christ's return, Satan will be bound in chains. He will be locked in hell, which is a bottomless pit, for a period of one thousand years. All of the wicked in hell will be shocked at his arrival. Isaiah the prophet wrote this about Satan being cast into hell:

> How you have fallen from heaven,
> Morning star, son of the dawn!
> You have been cast down to the earth,
> You who once laid low the nations!
> You said in your heart,
> "I will ascend to the heavens;
> I will raise my throne above the stars of God;
> I will sit enthroned on the mount of assembly,
> On the utmost heights of the sacred mountain.
> I will ascend above the tops of the clouds;
> I will make myself like the Most High."
> But you are brought down to the realm of the dead,
> To the depths of the pit (Isa 14:12-15).

At the end of the thousand years, Satan will be released from hell for a short season. He will stir up all of the wicked who are alive on the earth to rebel against Christ. There will be one last war where all of the wicked are destroyed. Human history upon the earth will come to an end. Then this is what the Bible says will happen to Satan: "And the devil, who deceived them, was cast into the lake of fire and brimstone where the beast and the false prophet are. And they will be tormented day and night forever and ever" (Rev 20:10, NKJV).

Do not be deceived. Satan has already been condemned and his power stripped from him through the death and resurrection of Jesus Christ. Satan knows that he and his angels cannot defeat God. He is, though, a great deceiver and would try to cause all of mankind to fear him. The truth is that he is the one who lives in fear of the day that he will receive judgment and be sentenced to eternity in the lake of fire.

This lesson is **important** because it teaches us the difference between hell and the lake of fire. It also makes clear that we do not need to fear Satan's power, for the Holy Spirit in us is greater than he is. Just as every person will be judged in the end, Satan will be judged too.

The **main truth** of this lesson is that Satan has already been defeated through the death and resurrection of Jesus Christ, God's Son. He knows what his judgment will be and he wants to take as many people to the lake of fire with him as possible.

Let's **review** what you have learned, by answering these questions:

1. Does Satan still retain his power and authority?
	A. If you said, "No, Satan's power and authority was stripped from him through the death and resurrection of Jesus Christ," then you are correct.

2. What will be the eternal punishment for Satan and his fallen angels?
	A. If you said that Satan and his fallen angels will be cast into the lake of fire, you are correct.

3. What is the difference between hell and the lake of fire?
	A. If you said hell is a temporary place and that the lake of fire is the eternal place of judgment, then you are correct.

Your **assignment** for this lesson is to listen to it at least three times, until you fully understand the difference between hell and the lake of fire. You should also be able to explain that Satan was judged and condemned through the death and resurrection of Jesus Christ and that his power and authority were stripped from him. Finally, you should be able to explain that Satan himself will receive eternal judgment and be cast alive into the lake of fire where he will be tormented for eternity.

Then share this teaching with fellow believers encouraging them not to fear Satan, but rather to become a witness to the lost, that they might be saved.

29 Eternal Judgment – Judgment of the Wicked

There is a town in Mexico named Tijuana. It is located right on the Mexican and USA border, across from the American city of San Diego, California. A very powerful drug lord lived in Tijuana. He was called "The Little Child." But his name was very deceiving. He led a drug gang that was very violent, murdering many people and selling illegal drugs. The government police had sought to capture this drug lord for many years. Finally, in the winter of 2010, the police got the lead that they were waiting for. The drug lord, known as the Little Child, would be in a particular house that evening.

A small army of police officers, armed with guns, descended on the house and arrested the drug lord. Also arrested with the drug lord were five of his gang leaders. But the big surprise was that there were also five corrupt police officers there in the house with the drug lord. They too were arrested. They all would be tried, found guilty, and sentenced to prison. It is really sad that the five corrupt police officers had to go to prison. The prison had not been built for police officers, but rather for criminals. But those five police officers had decided to follow the leadership of the drug lord. Thus, when they all were arrested, they would follow the drug lord "Little Child" to punishment in prison.

In the Bible, we read in the book of Hebrews that "it is appointed for men to die once, but after this comes the judgment" (Heb 9:27). Every person who has ever drawn a breath will one day stand before Jesus sitting upon his throne. On that day, everyone will be judged. The apostle John saw a vision of that judgment. This is what he wrote in his book, the Revelation:

> Then I saw a great white throne and him who was seated on it. The earth and the heavens fled from

his presence, and there was no place for them. And I saw the dead, great and small, standing before the throne, and books were opened. Another book was opened, which is the book of life. The dead were judged according to what they had done as recorded in the books. The sea gave up the dead that were in it, and death and Hades gave up the dead that were in them, and each person was judged according to what they had done. Then death and Hades were thrown into the lake of fire. The lake of fire is the second death. Anyone whose name was not found written in the book of life was thrown into the lake of fire" (Rev 20:11-15).

In our previous lessons you learned that there are two resurrections. The First Resurrection is for all believers. Every believer will be resurrected with a new immortal body that will never become sick, suffer pain, or die. But we also learned of the Second Resurrection. This is the resurrection of the wicked. They too will receive a body that will not die. Together, everyone will stand before the Great White Throne and be judged. At this judgment, books will be opened which will reveal everything a person has ever done—both the good and the bad.

There has been no perfect person except for Jesus Christ. Thus, everyone who stands before the throne should be condemned for the sins in their lives. Indeed, the apostle Paul wrote, "All have sinned and fall short of the glory of God" (Rom 3:23). But believers have nothing to fear on this day. All of our sins have been washed away—erased from the books of our lives. The Lord spoke through the prophet Isaiah and said,

"Come now, and let us reason together,"
Says the LORD,

"Though your sins are like scarlet,
They shall be as white as snow;
Though they are red like crimson,
They shall be as wool" (Isa 1:18, NKJV).

So, the books of the believers will record only the good deeds of their lives and their names will appear in the book of life. They will live forever with God as their Father. They will be joint heirs with Jesus Christ.

But for the unbelievers, those who were part of the Second Resurrection, things will not go well. Their books will reveal and make public every word and deed. Unfortunately, God will not weigh their good deeds against their bad deeds. This is not a school test where there is a minimum passing grade and if you get more questions correct than incorrect you pass. Paul wrote that "the wages of sin is death." James wrote "For whoever keeps the whole law and yet stumbles at just one point is guilty of breaking all of it" (James 2:10).

Thus, judgment before the Great White Throne is very straightforward. One has either sinned or not sinned. The blood of Jesus Christ has washed away all believers' sins. Therefore, believers stand before the Great White Throne as if they had never sinned. But the unbelievers will all stand condemned, because of the sins of their own lives. Their names will not be found written in the book of life. And they will be thrown into the lake of fire, where they will suffer great torment for eternity.

Many people argue that this punishment is unfair. After all, the lake of fire was created as a place of punishment for Satan and his fallen angels. In many ways, this eternal judgment is like what happened to the corrupt police officers in our story. The Mexican prison had not been built to imprison police officers. It had been built to punish lawbreakers like the drug lord and his gang. But when the five police officers became a part of the drug lord's gang, they became guilty of breaking the same laws. The very law that condemned the drug gang to prison, would also judge and condemn the corrupt police. Since unbelievers followed Satan into sin, they will also follow Satan into the eternal punishment of the lake of fire.

This lesson is **important** because it shows us again that the blood of Christ cleanses us from every sin. Believers need not fear the Great White Throne judgment; their names are written in the book of life.

The **main truth** of this lesson is that everyone who has ever lived will stand before the Great White Throne to be judged according to their works. When the books are opened, believers will have no sins recorded, and their names will be found in the book of life. Unbelievers' names will not be found, and they will be condemned because of their sins.

Answering these questions will help you remember the points of this lesson:

1. Who will stand before the Great White Throne to be judged?
    a. If you answered that everyone who has ever lived will stand before the Great White Throne, you answered correctly.

2. What is the eternal punishment for the unbelievers?
    A. If you said that all unbelievers will be cast into the lake of fire, you are right.

3. At the Great White Throne judgment, why are no sins found in the books of the believers?

A. If you said that the blood of Jesus has washed all of the believer's sins away, then you are correct.

Your **assignment** for this lesson is to listen to this lesson at least three times until you fully understand the Great White Throne judgment. Then share this teaching with fellow believers, encouraging them to testify to unbelievers so that the lost might be saved.

During this course, you have learned the six doctrines of the church which the writer of the Book of Hebrews states are the foundation doctrines.

The first foundation doctrine is repentance. Repentance is a change of direction in one's life. It always results in a change of behavior. Many people try to change their behavior on their own, but find themselves returning to the same old lifestyle. Godly sorrow brings about true repentance. And true repentance will always include the confession of sin. The Bible teaches us to humble ourselves and confess our sins to Christ. This is the starting point of true repentance. There will always be a change in the way a person thinks as part of repentance. Behavior that a person once thought was acceptable will now be seen as sin. Therefore, true repentance will result in a change of behavior which could include making restitution for offenses that have been done to others.

The second foundation doctrine is faith towards God. Faith is believing in God. Without faith, it is impossible to please God. Everyone must first believe that God exists and that he cares about the individual. True faith in God will result in miracles within the lives of the believer. You have also learned that it is through faith in Jesus Christ that one is saved and that salvation is not based upon a believer's works for God. But true faith will result in our doing work for God. Remember the apostle James said that "faith without works is dead."

The third foundation doctrine concerns baptisms. There is the baptism in water which every believer should take part of. It is the public testimony of one's decision to become a follower of Christ. After that, every believer should seek the baptism in the Holy Spirit with the initial evidence of speaking in other tongues. For it is through the baptism in the Holy Spirit that the believer receives power to be a witness. The final baptism is called the baptism in fire. This baptism is when God allows us to go through a time of testing and trial that refines our faith in him.

The fourth foundation doctrine is the laying on of hands. You have learned that Isaac laid hands on his sons to impart a blessing and that Moses laid hands on Joshua to impart authority. Spiritual gifts can also be imparted through the laying on of hands. Peter laid hands on people and they received the baptism of the Holy Spirit. People can receive healing when hands are laid upon them accompanied with prayer. Paul and Barnabas were ordained to missionary work when the leaders of the church of Antioch laid hands on them.

The fifth foundation doctrine concerns the resurrection of the dead. The Bible teaches us that there will be two resurrections. The first is the resurrection of the righteous and the second is the resurrection of the wicked. The first resurrection is three distinct events. The first resurrection event happened two thousand years ago when Jesus was resurrected from the dead. He is called the First Fruits of the resurrection, which is a proof that one day all believers will likewise be resurrected. The second event of the first resurrection will be the Rapture of the church. In a single moment, all of the dead in Christ will be resurrected from the dead. Immediately after that moment all believers who are alive will be transformed, receiving resurrected glorified bodies. The third and last event of the first resurrection will be when Christ returns to the earth at the end of the Tribulation. All the believers who came to the Lord during the Tribulation will be resurrected and changed. You have also learned about the second resurrection which is when the unbelievers will be resurrected from the dead so that they can stand before the Great White Throne to receive their eternal judgment.

This leads us to the sixth and final foundation doctrine, eternal judgment. We have learned that all authority flows from God the Father and that Jesus has been given all authority that he might judge the world. Every believer will stand before the Judgment Seat of Christ where their works and labors for Jesus will be judged and rewarded. You have learned that although God treats everyone equally in respect to salvation, every individual will receive their heavenly reward based upon what they have done for Christ. Satan also will be judged and receive eternal punishment. Hell is a temporary place of judgment reserved for unbelievers. The lake of fire is the eternal place of punishment that was created for Satan and his fallen angels. Unbelievers will also be cast into the lake of fire as their eternal punishment.

These six doctrines; Repentance, Faith, Baptisms, Laying on of Hands, Resurrection, and Eternal Judgment are the foundation doctrines that every believer should clearly understand.

Your final **assignment** for this course is to review the lessons as many times as is necessary to fully comprehend and know the six foundation doctrines of the church. You should be so proficient in this knowledge that you can easily teach it to new believers.